Joseph Pennell, Elizabeth Robins Pennell

Our Journey to the Hebrides

Joseph Pennell, Elizabeth Robins Pennell

Our Journey to the Hebrides

ISBN/EAN: 9783743316379

Manufactured in Europe, USA, Canada, Australia, Japa

Cover: Foto ©ninafisch / pixelio.de

Manufactured and distributed by brebook publishing software (www.brebook.com)

Joseph Pennell, Elizabeth Robins Pennell

Our Journey to the Hebrides

Our Journey to the Hebrides. By Joseph Pennell and Elizabeth Robins Pennell

NEW YORK: HARPER & BROTHERS, PRINTERS & PUBLISHERS, FRANKLIN SQUARE, MDCCCLXXXIX

Copyright, 1889, by HARPER & BROTHERS.

All rights reserved.

PREFACE.

The greater part of "Our Journey to the Hebrides" was published originally in Harper's Magazine. When it appeared it was severely criticised, and we were taken to task for not discovering in Scotland and the Scotch what has been made the fashion to find there—for not giving second-hand descriptions, which are the stock in trade of Scotch guide-books, whether romantic or real; in a word, for not staying at home and manufacturing our journey in the British Museum.

It is gradually dawning upon us that this is what is wanted by the majority of critics. To go to a country and tell what really happened to you—to dare to say, for the information of future cyclers or travellers, that one small piece of road is bad, that on one day out of ten or fifteen it rained, that at one small hotel you were uncomfortable or turned away, is enough to make the critic declare that you have found everything in that country to be awry. This was our fate when we attempted to describe the most enjoyable trip we ever made—our ride across France. We have no hesitation in saying that our trip to Scotland was the most miserable. We undertook to walk, owing to the misrepresentations of people who we do not believe ever in their lives walked half as far as we did a year ago. As we have shown, when tramping became unendurable we went by coach or train, by steamer or sail-boat; but we walked far enough to see the country as, we venture to think, it has seldom been seen by other travellers. For, with all its drawbacks, walking has this one advantage: not only do you stop at the correct show-places on your route, but you go slowly over the unknown country which lies between them. That the weather in the Western Highlands and Islands is vile is a fact which cannot be denied, though to mention it is held to be a crime. But, for the benefit of those who, because we speak of the rain and of the fatigue of walking, think we shut our eyes to everything else on our journey, let us say here, once and for all, that we found the whole country BEAUTIFUL and full of the most WONDERFUL EFFECTS; but we must also add that it is the most abominable to travel through, and its people are the most down-trodden on God's earth.

This is the best and most concise description of the Western Highlands and Islands that could be given.

Because we saw and described the actual condition of the population, and ignored the pleasures—

in which we might have joined—of a handful of landlords and sportsmen whose fathers brought about this condition, and who themselves are fighting to maintain it, we have been asked what is the use of digging up ancient history? Thank Heaven, it is now two years since the Crofters' Act was passed by Parliament; but when we were in the Islands the first test case of a tenant pleading against the landlord who wished to evict him was tried, and gained by the tenant. While we were in Barra, the disenfranchisement of the entire island was accomplished by a trick which the most unscrupulous American politician would not have dared to play. The Crofters' Commission had then just begun to reduce rents—fifty-seven per cent. is the average reduction—and to cancel arrears. It has raised rents on certain estates, is an argument used by landlords, who forget to tell you that where rents have been raised they have been compelled to give back pasture-land to the crofters. It was but a few weeks after our return to London that a rebellion broke out in the Island of Lewis, and was quelled only by the decision of the Edinburgh Court, which declared deer not to be protected by law; so that for the rest of the winter crofters and cotters ate venison with their oatmeal. It was this decision, and not the war-ships, which prevented open insurrection in all the Islands.

Some of our critics have been good enough to inform us that crofters were never turned off their crofts to make room for deer. With those who refuse to accept the testimony officially published in the Blue-books there is no use to enter into a discussion. For those who know little of the subject, and for whom Blue-books would necessitate long study, here are the facts—facts which no one can question—in a nutshell. We quote from an article on "The Crofters of the Highlands," published in the *Westminster Review* for February, 1888:

> "In addition to these many injustices" (injustices, that is, suffered by the crofters), "there is one which in certain districts almost overshadows them all; namely, the absorption of vast areas, embracing much fertile land in deer forests. It matters little whether crofters were actually evicted to make room for deer, or whether sheep farms have been converted to this purpose; both have happened very largely, with the result that, according to the Royal Commissioners, about two million acres are now devoted to deer forests. Large as this figure is, it is considerably below the mark, as has been shown by even better authorities on the subject. Nor must it be supposed that deer forests consist merely of barren and worthless land. Unless there is a large amount of good grass-land in a forest the deer would starve, and all this good land in times past supported a large population, whose descendants are now suffering destitution in the bare and unfruitful regions near the coast."

To their shame be it said, the American millionaires who are beginning to rent these deer forests are the men who are now doing the most to encourage the continuance in their present position of the sons of the land-grabbers, or, we should say, the heroes of the ancient history and romance of the country.

There is another evil of these great deer forests which should not be forgotten. A crofter, after working all day, often has to sit up all night to keep these beasts, which were supposed to be private property, out of his little croft. For if the deer eat all his crops, he had no redress; if the crofter shot one of them, or hurt it in any way in driving it out, you may be sure the factor made him suffer for it—at one time he would most likely have been evicted. We want it to be understood that in these vast tracts of deer forest none but sportsmen and game-keepers are allowed to go. If your house were to lie on one side and the village on the other, you would have to go miles around to reach it. Nor can you go near streams which run in the open country, for fear you may disturb the fish, which are preserved for English or American sportsmen.

Just as we are writing this Preface we have begun to receive, for the first time in our lives, anonymous letters. Hitherto we did not believe there were people stupid and imbecile enough to write such things. One of these creatures, who is ashamed of his own identity, encloses, with an amusing letter written on Kansas City Club paper—which, however, does not reveal whether he is the president or the hall porter of the club—an article of a column and a half from the *Scotsman*, which calls our "Journey to the Hebrides" "sentimental nonsense," "culpable misrepresentation," "amazing impertinence." And then, without attempting to show in what the misrepresentation or nonsense or impertinence consists, the writer of this article goes on to give his own ideas on the subject of the crofters, quoting statements made from other sources, and attributing them to us, misrepresenting us, and yet not attempting to contradict any one fact brought forward in any one of the articles, but taking up space in the paper to contradict the reports of the *Scotsman's* own reporter, printed but a few months before. We are accused of exaggerating the misery of the people. We have lying by our side as we write, column after column, amounting to page after page, from the *Scotsman*, which is by no means the crofters' friend, giving detailed pictures of this misery, which we, in our generalizing, could not approach. Here is a specimen taken at hazard from the pile of clippings. "A Tale of Poverty" it is headed, and it was published January 17, 1888:

"Quite a typical case of poverty was that of Donald Mackenzie, a middle-aged man, who occupied a half croft at a rental of £2. He was married, with five young children, and they had been living exclusively on potatoes, occasionally with fish, for three months, until they got a half boll of meal from a destitution fund. That was now done, and he had that day borrowed a bowlful from a neighbour. He had fished at Stornoway in the summer, and had kept the family alive; but his wife assured the stranger that he had not brought home a single shilling. She added that she herself had not had shoes for four years, and the children were no better off. A very similar case was that of Norman Macmillan. He was a cottar and fisherman, having a half lot from another tenant. He had also not taken home a shilling from the fishing last year; and, except working on his lot, he could find nothing to do until the fishing season came on again. He had seven children, the eldest twelve years. They had eaten up their potatoes by the beginning of winter, and now they had but a little barley-meal left. He did not know what to do now, he said, unless Providence opened the way for them. They had often been without food, he said, although they had kept it. There was none to relieve them. He stated that formerly they used to get credit from the merchants while they were engaged at the fishing, but that they did not get now. One of the houses visited in this township was that of the wife of Donald Macmillan, one of the men now standing trial in Edinburgh on a charge of having taken part in the Park deer raid. Macmillan lived in a very small cot at the back of his father's house, which his father had used as a barn. It was very poorly furnished even for that locality. There was a family of five small children, and there was only one bed in the house, with one blanket. Three of the children slept out with a neighbour. Macmillan cultivated the half of his father's croft, and had one cow. He was also a fisherman, having a share in a boat of forty-one feet keel; but, though he had attended the Barra fishing last summer, he had made nothing. His wife had got a boll of meal from the destitution fund, but besides that, she had only two barrels of potatoes. Previous to getting that meal, they had lived exclusively on potatoes. She stated that when her husband went out to the deer raid, there was but one barrel of potatoes; but since then, she explained, she had fallen back upon the seed."

Here is another, from January 20th of the same year, when four columns were devoted to crofter affairs:

"From here a drive of about four miles brought the visitors to Arebruich—a township fixed in a spot which was surely never intended for human beings. As one passes onwards from Balallan, the soil gradually sinks lower and lower on the north side of the loch until, when Arebruich is reached, it is almost level to the water's edge. The result is that the land is literally a floating bog, and it is a miracle how the poor people, who labour away at the barren scraps of earth which show some signs of cultivation, manage to get any food raised out of them. A rude, clayish pathway extends for some little distance from the main road, but it soon stops, as if the builders had thrown up the work in disgust. There are sixteen crofts, such as they are, in the township, and these are occupied by twenty-six families. The first house visited was that of John Mackinnon, a stout, good-looking man in spite of his surroundings. He lives on his mother's lot, which is rented at £2.15s., exclusive of taxes. His mother, who is eighty years old, lives, along with an unmarried daughter, in an adjoining house. He paid 35s. two years ago to the factor, but since then he has been able to pay nothing. He fished as a hired man last year at Lybster; but his earnings were so small that when his season's board was paid he had only 9d. left. A friend had to lend him his passage-money. At present he has three barrels of potatoes left, but neither meal nor money. He has two of a family, besides himself and wife. They have to live on potatoes. His mother never got any parochial relief, and she and her daughter have to struggle along as best they can. He has one cow and eight sheep. When the destitution meal was being distributed he got three stones, and his mother an equal quantity. He does not know what to do, and has no prospects whatever. The next house presented a worse case. It was that of Widow Murdo Macleod, a sister of Mackinnon. She said her husband was drowned at Loch Seaforth seven years ago, when they were only ten months married. She had one daughter, who was born shortly after her husband was drowned. She has made her living all these years by knitting and sewing and odd jobs, but never got any help from the Parochial Board, though she applied several times. She has neither land nor stock, and never had any. She generally gets a few potatoes from her brother at harvest time. She has half a barrel on hand at present, and about a stone of meal, the remains of what was got from the destitution fund. She always tried to be industrious, and therefore was never actually in absolute want. She always enjoyed good health, and felt very thankful for it. The hut in which this woman and her daughter live is wretchedly poor, and the single bed is barely covered with a thin blanket."*

On January 20th, in a leader, the same paper declared that the facts which we have given are "distressing," and ought to excite "interest" and sympathy. There is no talk here of sentimental nonsense! Distressing we should think they were. One cannot help saying that it is nothing less than infamous that a mere handful of landlords should have controlled the destiny of, and extracted every penny from, the population of these Islands — the people whom they have kept for generations in poverty, not that they might improve the land, but that they might pass their own time in useless idleness and cruel sport. It is not a question of over-population. The real evil is that the Islanders have been ground down and tyrannized over simply to gratify the amusements of their masters. We have heard again and again that the position of a landlord does not pay; if it did not, the landlords would sell their estates to-morrow.

For weeks, early in this year (1888), every Scotch and English paper, even to the *Times*, had columns about the misery of the crofters—that is, columns of extracts similar to these we have quoted. Whatever reasons were given for it, no one questioned their destitution. And yet within a year all these reports are forgotten; and for generalizing and not

---

* See note at the end of Preface.

going into details—heart-breaking details—we are called sickly sentimentalists. So glaring is this complete forgetfulness and contradiction that we cannot help taking some notice of it, and calling the attention of these papers to their own reports.

As to the rest of our critics, they did not even know enough to contradict themselves, except in one case, which we have pointed out elsewhere, and their other criticism is not directed against our facts.

In dwelling upon the misery of the people, we do not pretend, as has been suggested, to give an off-hand settlement of the economic problems of the Islands. We merely state what we saw, what it was impossible to avoid seeing, wherever we went. It must be remembered that it is not merely a minority, or even a majority, but the entire population who exist in this condition of absolute wretchedness and semi-starvation. With the exception of a few small towns on the coast for the convenience of tourists and landlords, you find throughout the Islands but the occasional beautiful castle or shooting-lodge, or great farm-house, and the many crowded stone piles politely called cottages. And it was because we were more struck with this misery than with the romance of the past that, our journey over, we interested ourselves in learning something of the immediate reasons for the present condition of the Western Highlanders and Islanders, rather than in reading about the murders and massacres of the MacGregor and the Macleod, the Mac this and the Mac that. We were not blind to the beauty, the sternness, the wildness of the country; but the sadness and sorrows of its people impressed us even more than the wonder and beauty of their land.

JOSEPH PENNELL.
ELIZABETH ROBINS PENNELL.

WESTMINSTER, *November* 20, 1888.*

---

* Even while we revise this Preface more news comes from the Island of Lewis. On Lady Matheson's estates rents have been reduced 42 and 53 per cent., and arrears cancelled 84 and 91 per cent. This is from the *Times* of December 20th:

"CROFTERS' RENTS.—The Crofter Commission yesterday issued their first decisions in relation to Lady Matheson's property in the Island of Lewis, the centre of the land agitation last winter. They have granted an average reduction of 42 per cent. on the rental of 150 crofter tenants in the parish of Barvas, on the west side of Lewis. The arrears of rent due, which was a striking feature in Lewis, have been cancelled to the extent of 84 per cent. Of a total of £2422, the Commissioners have cancelled £2043."

If there had not been injustice before, is it probable that there would now be such wholesale reductions and cancellings? We suppose it is *sentimentalism* to record these facts.

CHRISTMAS-DAY, 1888.

CONTENTS.

	PAGE
IN THE HIGHLANDS .	3
ON THE ISLANDS .	83
TO THE EAST COAST, AND BACK AGAIN.	167

ILLUSTRATIONS.

	PAGE
Crofters' Cottages near Uig, Skye	*Frontispiece*
Vignette for First Paper	1
Tarbet, Loch Lomond	11
Glencroe	15
Loch Restil	21
Inverary	23
Cross at Inverary	29
Scotland and the Hebrides	31
Kilchrennan	37
Loch Leven, from Ballachulish	41
Oban	43
Coast of Mull	53
Ross of Mull, looking towards Iona	59
Headland of Gribun, from Ulva	65
"One of his Strange Things Happened"	77
Vignette for Second Paper	81
In the Transept of the Cathedral, Iona	85
Iona	87
Tomb of Macleod	90
Castle Bay, from Barra	103

Town of Barra	109
Mountains of Harris, from Tarbet	113
Gathering Peat	125
The "Dunara Castle"	131
Interior of a Weaver's Cottage	135
Doing Skye	141
A real Highland Lassie	147
Dunvegan Castle	153
Graveyard of the Macleod	156
Tail-piece	163
Vignette for Third Paper	165
Fisher-boats hauled up near Buckie	183
The only Castle I drew	186
Near Cullen	187
Bit of Macduff	190
Near Banff	193
Banff, from Macduff	195
Fraserburgh	199
In the Harbor, Fraserburgh	203
Gutters at Work, Fraserburgh	207
Coming Home from the Fisheries, Fraserburgh	211
Entrance to the Harbor at Montrose	215
Ruins at Arbroath	221

IN THE HIGHLANDS.

We never looked forward to a pleasure trip with so much misery as we did to our journey to the Hebrides. We wanted a holiday.

"Go to Scotland," suggested the editor of Harper's.

"Let us rather wander through unexplored France," we proposed, in a long letter, though we had already explored it for ourselves more than once.

"Scotland would be better," was the answer in a short note.

"But why not let us discover unknown Holland?" we asked, as if it had not been discovered a hundred times already.

"Scotland would be better," was still the answer, and so to Scotland we went.

It was a country about which we cared little, and knew less. We had heard of Highlands and Lowlands, of Melrose and Stirling, but for our lives we could not have pointed them out on the map. The rest of our knowledge was made up of confused impressions of Hearts of Mid-Lothian and

Painters' Camps in the Highlands, Macbeths and Kidnappers, Skye terriers and Shetland shawls, blasted heaths and hills of mist, Rob Roys and Covenanters; and, added to these, positive convictions of an unbroken Scotch silence and of endless breakfasts of oatmeal, dinners of haggis, and suppers of whiskey. Hot whiskey punch is a good thing in its way, and at times, but not as a steady diet. Oatmeal we think an abomination. And as for haggis—well, we only knew it as it was once described to us by a poet: the stomach of some animal filled with all sorts of unpleasant things and then sewed up. We recalled the real dinners and friendly peasants of France and Italy, and hated the very name of Scotland.

It will easily be understood that we could not plan a route out of our ignorance and prejudice. It remained to choose a guide, and our choice, I hardly know why, fell upon Dr. Johnson. Every one must remember—I say this though we did not even know it until we looked into the matter—that Dr. Johnson met Boswell in Edinburgh, and in his company journeyed up the east coast as far as Inverness, then across the Highlands to the west, and so to the Hebrides, coming back by way of Inverary, Loch Lomond, and Glasgow. It looked a long journey on the map, and seemed a weary one in the pages of Boswell and Johnson;

but as if this were not bad enough, we made up our minds, for the sake of novelty, to walk.

Of our preparations for the journey I will say nothing. We carried less than Stanley and more than the average tramp. We took many things which we ought not to have taken, and we left behind many things which we ought to have taken. But this matters little, since our advice to all about to start on a walking tour is, *Don't*.

On the 28th of July we arrived in

EDINBURGH,

"a city too well known to admit description." If Dr. Johnson thought so a hundred years ago, it is not for us, who propose to be his followers, to differ from him. Indeed, during our stay in that city, so eager were we to be faithful to him in all things that we should have allowed ourselves to be dined, teaed and suppered, even as he was, but for an obstacle. The only person whom we knew in Edinburgh was away, and the fame of our coming had not, as with Dr. Johnson, gone before us.

We were careful to find St. James's Court, where Boswell lived, and where clothes, drying in what sun there is, now hang from his windows. And we went to the old White Horse Inn, where the Doctor, on his arrival, stayed until Boswell came to carry him off in triumph; and where probably the tourist of another year will not go, for already in the court-yard are signs of the coming of the destroyer.

We had resolved to reverse the order of their journey by going to the Western Islands first, and coming home along the east coast. In this way we should avoid the September storms which kept them in the Hebrides. Now we also decided to go straight to Glasgow, and not to stop at Hamilton, where they spent a night.

On Saturday, July 30th, we began our walk in a cab, and continued it for many miles in a railway-carriage. We represented to ourselves that the country between Edinburgh and Glasgow, of which we knew nothing, was stupid, and that we must get to Glasgow for Sunday. There was no earthly reason for this, but it was an excuse, and we made the most of it.

Dr. Johnson says that "to describe a city so much frequented as

GLASGOW

is unnecessary," and again we are willing to take his word for it. But its Cathedral was the first of the many surprises Scotland had in store for us. We had heard of it, but that was all. One young lady of Glasgow, fresh from a tour on the Continent, told us that she had never seen it. We were therefore prepared to find it no great thing. The exterior did not disappoint our expectations, but we have seldom been more impressed with an interior, and this though we had just come from the loveliest churches of England.

The crypt, or rather the under church, is its pride, as indeed it well may be. A verger stood smoking a pipe at the south door, and we told him what we thought. J——, after three years' work in the English cathedrals, felt himself no mean authority.

"It's the finest in the world," said the verger.

"In Great Britain perhaps, but not in Europe," said J——; for we had been but a moment before comparing it, as it now is, a cold, bare, show-place, to the under church of Assisi with the frescos on the walls, the old lamps burning before altars, the sweet smell of incense, and the monks kneeling in prayer.

"I only tell you what those *qualified* have said," and the verger settled the matter and J——'s pretensions.

It was in the Glasgow crypt Rob Roy gave the warning to Frank Osbaldistone. The guide-book recalled the incident, which we had forgotten. Indeed the farther we went, the more we were reminded that to travel in Scotland is to travel through the Waverley Novels, and that these to us were but a name. Since our return we have tried to read them again, to be quite honest, with but indifferent pleasure. We are so wanting in appreciation that we find Scott's description of the crypt stupid, and we are not thrilled by the daring deeds of the MacGregor.

The Art Gallery in Glasgow was no less a surprise to us than the Cathedral. Its catalogue contains more Titians, Rembrandts, Hobbemas, and other great masters than any other in Europe. But if we wondered at the catalogue, we were still more astonished when we came to see the pictures!

We stayed in Glasgow until Monday morning, when we again took the train, but this time for a few miles only. We bought tickets for Kilpatrick, and a sharp lookout we had to keep for it from the carriage windows. At the stations, no one called the names, which, in true British fashion, were less easy to find than that of the best brand of mustard or of the best hotel in Glasgow. At Kilpatrick, when I pulled my head in after the usual search, J—— was already at the opposite door. He did not care where he was, he said; he would get out. In the distance, we could see Dumbarton Rock rising from the plain against a blue sky. Here, as in our plans for the day's journey, it was the one prominent landmark.

Kilpatrick is said to have been the birthplace of St. Patrick. I do not know what authority Black* has for the legend; certainly not that of the vil-

---

* Not William, but the guide-book Black.

lagers. St. Patrick was no British man, one of them told us; and, moreover, he never lived in Kilpatrick, but on the hill. But had we ever heard of Captain Shonstone, the hairbor-maister? He was a great man.

We made a great show of briskness by going the long way round by the canal. This was the only time throughout our journey that we turned from the main road—except to take a short-cut. Mr. Lee Meriwether, in his Tramp Abroad, thought it an advantage of walking that he could leave the road to see whatever was to be seen near, but not from it. For our part, after the first mile, we never took an extra step for any sight; that is, whenever our knapsacks were on our backs. At Dumbarton we did not even climb the rock, though Dr. Johnson walked to the very top. Instead, we lunched and talked politics with the British workman in a coffee tavern.

After Dumbarton, we left the Clyde to follow the Leven. It was just beyond the town we first saw Ben-Lomond, a blue shadow on the horizon when the clouds were heavy above; a high bare mountain, seamed and riven, when the sun shone upon it. We lost sight of it in a succession of long, stupid villages; on the shady road, where the trees met overhead, we could see it again through the net-work of branches. Clouds were low on its heights, and a veil of soft light rain fell before it when, having left our knapsacks in the inn at Balloch, we rowed up the Leven, a little quiet river between low woods and flat meadow-land, to

LOCH LOMOND.

It was the first Scotch lake we saw, and we thought it very like any other lake.

We were off by eight in the morning. It was clear and cool, like an October day at home. Our road lay for a while close to the loch, then turned and went round the parks and lawns that sloped gently to the shore, so that it was only over a stone wall or through a gap in the hedge we could see the blue water and the wooded islands. We were now on the fighting-ground of the Colquhoun and the MacGregor, we learned from Black, who—we know it to our cost—is a better guide to the romance and history of Scotland than to its roads. It is but poor comfort when you ask for a good route to be given a quotation.

Rob Roy is the hero of Loch Lomond, and if you cross—as we did not—to the other side, you may see his cave and his prison and a lot of his other belongings. But I think that which is best worth seeing on the loch is the Colquhoun's village of Luss, with its neat, substantial cottages and trim gardens. In the Highlands you can have your fill of tales of outlaws and massacres and horrors; but it is not every day you come to a

TARBET, LOCH LOMOND.

village like this, where men are allowed to live a little better than their beasts.

At the Colquhoun Arms in Luss we ate our lunch, and that was our undoing. It left us in a mood for lounging, and we had still eight miles to go. We found it harder work the second day than the first. Our knapsacks weighed like lead, and did not grow lighter; each mile seemed interminable. This was the more provoking because with every step the way grew lovelier. Almost all the afternoon we were within sight of the loch, while on our left the mountains now rose from the very road-side, and hedges gave place to hill-sides of ferns and heather-patched bowlders. Used as we both were to cycling, the slowness and monotony of our pace was intolerable. We longed for a machine that would carry us and our knapsacks with ease over the hard, dustless road. For one mile we tried to keep each other in countenance. J—— was the first to rebel openly. The Highlands were a fraud, he declared; the knapsack was an infernal nuisance and he was a fool to carry it. About three miles from Tarbet he sat down and refused to go any farther.

Just then, by chance, there came a drag full of young girls, and when they saw us they laughed, and passed by on the other side. And likewise a dog-cart, and the man driving, when he first saw us, waved his hand, taking us to be friends; but when he was at the place and looked at us, he also passed by on the other side. But two tricyclers, as they journeyed, came where we were; and when they saw us they had compassion on us, and came to us, and gathered up our knapsacks and set them on their machines and brought them to the inn and took care of them. And yet there are many who think cyclers nothing but cads on casters!

To tell the truth, had these two men been modern Rob Roys, we would have yielded up our knapsacks as cheerfully; nor would we have sorrowed never to see them again.

As we went on our way lightly and even gayly, we came to the inn at

TARBET,

and were received by a waiter in a dress-coat. It was a big hotel low down by the loch, with Ben-Lomond for opposite neighbor. The company at dinner was made up of Englishmen and Englishwomen. But everybody talked to everybody else. An Englishman, it seems, becomes civilized in the Highlands. There, those he sits down with at dinner, as is the way with Frenchmen, are his friends; at home, he would look upon them as his enemies.

After dinner we went to walk with the cyclers. As a great theatrical moon came sailing up

GLENCROE.

through the sky behind Ben-Lomond, one told us in broad Scotch how from the Jungfrau he had once watched the moon rise, and at the sight had bur-r-r-st into tee-eers. But just then, had I wept at all, it must have been from sheer weariness, so I turned my back upon the beauty of the evening and went to bed.

It was well on towards noon the next day before we were on our way.

"It looks like business," said a young lady feeding a pet donkey, as she saw us start.

"It feels like it too," said I, dolefully, for the knapsacks were no lighter, and our feet were tender after the sixteen miles of the day before.

It was two easy miles to Arrochar, a village of white cottages and a couple of inns, one with a tap, the other with a temperance sign. Here we were ferried across Loch Long by a fisherman sad as his native hills. It was a wretched season, he told us; there were few people about. On the west side of the loch, the road was wild, and soon turned up to Glencroe. At the lower end of the pass, sheep browsed on the hill-sides, and in tiny fields men and women were cutting grass. The few cottages were new. But these things we left behind when the road began to wind upward in short, sudden curves. It was shut in on both sides by mountains; the sun glittered on their sheer precipices and overhanging cliffs and on the hundreds of watercourses with which their slopes were seamed. The way was steep, and I thought I should have died before I reached the top. At the last we made a short-cut up to the stone known, out of compliment to Wordsworth, as "Rest and be Thankful." There may be men and women with so much poetry in their souls, that after that stiff climb they will still care to find the appropriate lines in their guide-books, and then have breath enough left to repeat them. But we were too hot and tired to do anything but lie on the grass and, as we rested, look down upon and enjoy the wonderful pictures away beyond and below us.

In this lonely place a little loch lies dark and peaceful among the hills. Restil, its name is; I do not know what it means, but it has a pretty sound. Nothing could be more monotonous, to tramp over than the long stretch of road which follows Kinglas Water almost to the shores of Loch Fyne. Our feet were blistered, and now ached at every step. Our shoulders were sorely strained. The things we said are best not written. When the coach from Inverary passed and until it was out of sight, we made a feint of not being tired. But the rest of the way we now grew eloquent in abuse, now limped in gloomy silence.

It was a mistake (which we afterward regretted) going to

CAIRNDOW,

and I do not know why we made it, except that in mapping out our route we had little help from Black. We had to learn from experience, which is but a poor way, if you find out your errors when it is too late to mend them. We were bound to Inverary, Dr. Johnson's next stopping-place. At the top of Glencroe, we should have turned to our left and walked down Hell's Glen to St. Catharine's, where there is a steam ferry to Inverary on the opposite shores of Loch Fyne. As it was, we had turned to our right and walked to a point almost at the top of the loch where there was no ferry, and where five miles lay between us and St. Catharine's. This was the coach road from Tarbet, and the guide-book has but little interest in travellers who go afoot. Though one hears much of walking tours in the Highlands, but few are made. In seven weeks' walking we scarcely met even a tramp.

We felt our mistake the more keenly because of the unpleasantness of the inn. The landlady greeted us warmly; like the ferry-man of the morning, she found there were too few tourists abroad. But her greeting was better than her rooms or her dinner, and she herself was unco' canny.

There was in the inn a young artist whose name she told us. We had never heard it, and this showed our ignorance; for he came from London, where he had won the first prize in an exhibition, and his wife, who was with him, had won the second, and altogether they were very great, and it was small wonder they did not care to dine with unknown travellers who carried sketch-books. But, indeed, I think in no country in the world except Great Britain will one artist not be glad to meet another when chance throws them together. An English artist wrecked on a desert island would not recognize a brother artist in the same plight as "one of the fraternity," unless the latter could make good his claims by the excellence, not of his work, but of his letters of introduction or the initials after his name. Nor does he unbend in the Highlands, where Englishmen of other crafts become so very sociable.

When we walked out after a bad dinner, the eastern hills rose against the pale yellow light of the coming moon. One star sent a shining track across the dark water, over which every now and again the wind marked its passage in long lines of silver ripples. Of all the sweet still evenings of our journey, we shall always remember this as the sweetest and stillest.

It was in the morning that the landlady showed her canniness. She sent us off in her boat to be

LOCH RESTIL.

rowed across the loch; this, she said, we should find the shorter way to Inverary. But on the water one of the boys let slip the truth. We should have half the distance to walk if we went straight from Cairndow to St. Catharine's, there to cross by the steam ferry. Judge of our righteous wrath! When they rowed us back to the

INVERARY.

Cairndow side, the boys were careful to land us a good quarter of a mile below the inn. The worst of it was that once on shore again, we did not know whom to believe, the mother or the children. We were in a fine state of doubt, until a woman in the first cottage we came to reassured us. This was by far the shorter way, and we need not hurry, she added; we could not help reaching St. Catharine's in time for the ferry at eleven.

She was right. It seemed a short walk by the loch. We stopped only once, that J—— might get an old ruin on the very water's edge. When we came to St. Catharine's we had an hour or more to sit at the inn door. It was one of those hot, misty days, which are not rare during the short Highland summer. The mountains were shrouded in a burning white haze. The loch was like glass. On its opposite shore, Inverary, white and shining, was reflected in its waters; and close by, at the foot of the hills, the turreted castle of the Argylls stood out strongly against the dark wood.

Here we made up our minds to go to Dalmally by coach. It was much too hot to walk. This left us free to take a nearer look at the castle, which, when we saw how painfully it had been restored, we thought less fine. In the town itself, though there is plenty sketchable, there is nothing notable, save the old town-cross, with its weather-worn carvings, which stands upon the shore, with loch and hills for background.

After lunch at the Argyll Arms, suddenly an excursion steamer and the coach from Tarbet poured streams of tourists into the place. Two more coaches dashed out from the hotel stables. The wide street was one mass of excursionists and landlords and waiters, and coachmen in red coats and gray beavers, and guards with bundles and boxes. There was a short, sharp struggle for seats, and in the confusion we came off with the best, and found ourselves on the leading coach, whirling from the glare of the loch, through the cool shade of a wooded glen, to the stirring sounds of the "Standards on the Braes of Mar," shouted by a party of Lowland Sandies who filled the other seats.

At the first pause, the coachman pointed to deer standing quietly under the graceful silver birches that shut in the road.

"Shush-sh-sh-sh!" screamed the Sandies, in a new chorus.

"Why canna ye put salt on their tails?" cried one.

Though later, cows and sheep and ducks fled before their noise, the deer never stirred. And yet, I suppose, in the season the Duke of Argyll and his guests come stalking these tame creatures, and call it sport.*

---

* It is for this supposition we have already been taken so severely to task and laughed at for our imagined ignorance of the difference between roe deer and red deer. We are glad to have afforded the critics amusement; but we have since looked into the matter, and a friend, a Highlander who knows the Highlands as well as if not better than any of our critics, assures us there are red deer in these woods. So much for that wild burst of criticism! But if this were not

All that afternoon, through the woods of Glenaray and across the purple moorland beyond, afar over the banks and braes and streams around, there rang out the strong voice of Sandy off for a holiday. Highland valleys were filled with the pathetic strains of

> "We started up a candy shop, John,
> But couldna make it pay,
> John Anderson, my jo!"

Highland hills re-echoed the burden of a loving father's song:

> "For she's my only daughter,
> 'Tis I myself that taught her
> To wear spangled clothes
> And twirl round on her toes,
> And her name it was Julia McNaughter."

Between songs there were jokes, as at the minstrels.

"Ta-ta, James; au revore," they called to men mowing in the meadows.

"And havna ye a letter for us?" they asked the old woman at a lonely post-office.

To a beggar by the way-side they gave witticisms with their pennies:

> "Canna ye sing a Gaelic song?"
> "Canna ye stand on your head?"
> "He's a Grecian!"

---

the case, our supposition would not have been unnatural when certain aspects of British sport are considered — the hunting in Epping Forest, the performances of her Majesty's stag-hounds, for example!

If the point of their jokes is not very clear, the fault is not mine; I am trying to be not witty, but realistic.

There was one in the party — a woman, of course—who remembered duty.

"Isn't it bonny country?" she kept asking. "And what's yon bonny glen, my laddie?" and she poked the guard.

"And Sandy, mon, ye're nae lookin' at the scenery," she said to her husband.

"Toot, I clean forgot the scenery," and Sandy broke off in his singing to stare through his fieldglass at a bare hill-side.

Almost within sight of Loch Awe we came to a hill that was so steep we all left the coach and walked a couple of miles up the shadeless hot road. An objection sometimes made to cycling is that it is half walking; but in the Highlands you would walk less if you rode a cycle than if you travelled by coach. From the top of the hill we looked down to where, far below, lay Loch Awe and its many islands. In this high place, with the beautiful broad outlook, gypsies had camped. I never yet knew the Romany who did not pitch his tent in the loveliest spot for miles around.

We had no definite plan for the night. We left it to chance, and we could not have done better. At the station at Dalmally we said goodby to our friends, who went gayly to another bonny glen, and we took the train for Loch Awe. It hurried us round the top of the loch in a few minutes to Loch Awe station, where on the platform were crowds of men in conventional tweed knickerbockers and Norfolk jackets, and women in jockey caps and fore-and-afts; and moreover, there were pipers with their pipes under their arms. From the carriage window we had seen the Loch Awe hotel, perched high on the hill-side, and looking down to the gray ivy-grown ruins of Kilchurn. It seemed no place for tourists who carried their baggage on their backs. But hardly had we left the carriage, when up stepped an immaculate creature in blue coat and brass buttons to tell us, with his cap in his hand, that our telegram had been received and the Port Sonachan boat was in waiting. That from all that elegant crowd of travellers he should have picked us out, the only two in the least disreputable-looking and travel-worn, showed, we thought, his uncommon discrimination. If, without knowing it, we had telegraphed to a hotel of which we had never heard, if in consequence a private steam-yacht was now at our disposal, why should we hesitate? Indeed, we had not time, for immediately a sailor seized our shabby knapsacks and carried them off with as much respect as if they had been Saratoga trunks. We followed him into a little yacht, which we graciously shared with an

Englishman, his wife, two children, eleven bags, and three bath-tubs.

The man in the blue coat kindly kept his boat at the pier until J—— had made quite a decent note

CROSS AT INVERARY.

of Kilchurn Castle. It has its legends, but it is not for me to tell them. Mr. Hamerton, who has written poetry about it and ought to know, declares they are not to be told in prose. Then we steamed down the loch, past the islands, one with a lonely graveyard, another with a large house; past the high mountains shutting in the Pass of Brander, to a hotel perfect of its kind. It stood on a little promontory of its own. A bay-window in the dining-room commanded the view north, south, and west over the loch. As we ate our dinner we could watch the light slowly fade and the hills darken against it. The dinner was excellent, and the people at table were friendly. There was a freedom about the house that made us think of Dingman's Ferry in its best days, of the Water Gap before its splendor came upon it, of Bar Harbor before it was exploited. It was not a mere place of passage, like the hotels at Tarbet and at Loch Awe; but those who came to it stayed for their holiday. All the men were there for the fishing, which is good, and most of them, tired after their day's work, came to dinner in their fishing clothes. Their common sport made them sociable. They were kind to us, but in their kindness was pity that we too were not fishermen. The landlord, who was a Cameron, was neither great nor obsequious. He had interest for this man's salmon and that man's trout, and good counsel for our journeying. He had been game-keeper for many years on the shores of Loch Awe, which he knew and loved. He had seen Mr. Hamerton, and his boats and his painter's camp. Since we have been to Loch Awe

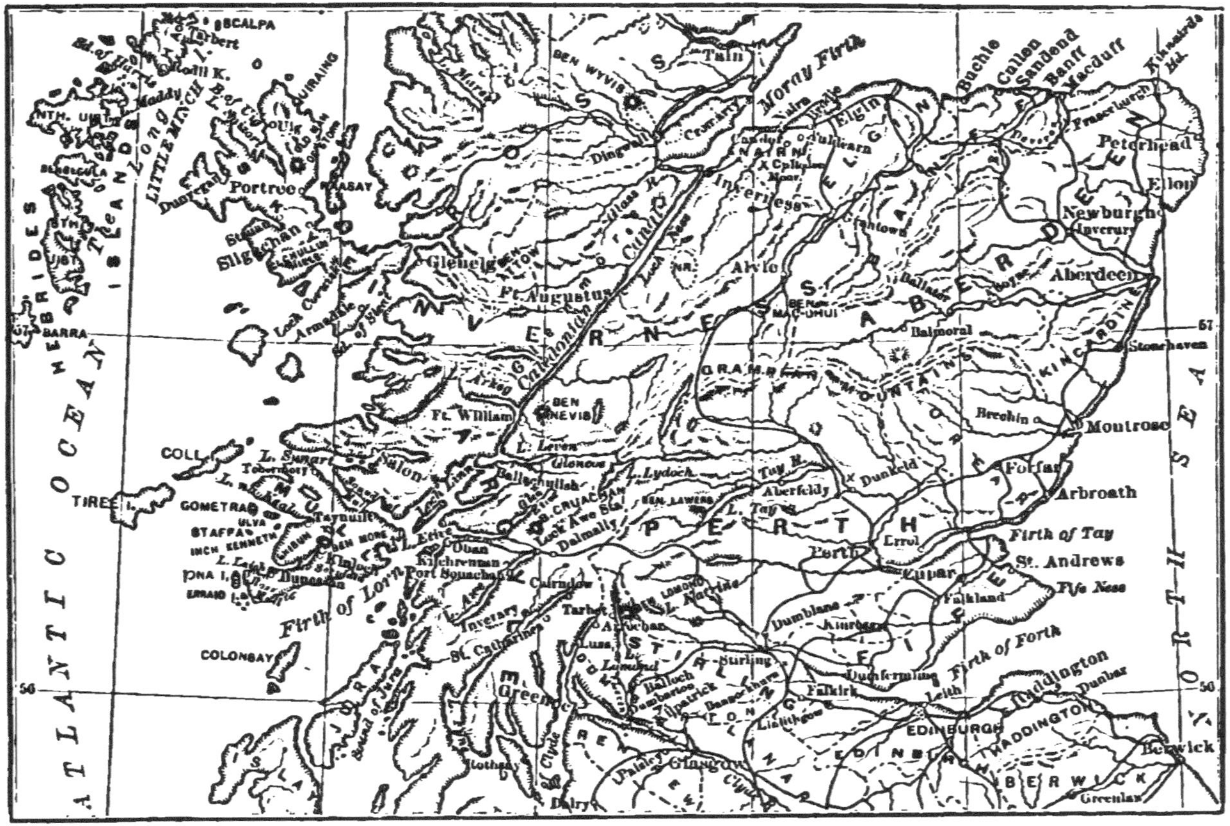

SCOTLAND AND THE HEBRIDES.

we have had an admiration for Mr. Hamerton which his book about it never gave us. Seldom do men show greater love for beauty in their choice of a home than he did, when he set up his tent on the island of the dead. As his books show, he is sufficient unto himself. Before the first month had ended, many might have wearied for other company save that of the hills and the water, the dead and a madman.

We left Port Sonachan in the morning. Mr. Cameron walked down to his pier with us, and a Duncan rowed us across to South Port Sonachan, where there is another hotel, and where we took the road to Loch Etive. Again the morning was hot and misty. In the few fields by the way men and women were getting in the hay, and the women, in their white sacks and handkerchiefs about their heads, looked not unlike French peasants. On each hill-top was a group of Highland cattle, beautiful black and tawny creatures, standing and lying in full relief against the sky. Two miles, a little more or less, brought us to a village wandering up and down a weed-grown, stone-covered hill-side. To our left a by-road climbed to the top of the hill, past the plain, bare kirk, with its little graveyard, and higher still to two white cottages, their thatched roofs green with a thick growth of grass, and vines growing about their doors, the loch and the mountain in the background.

But the cottages, which to the right of our road straggled down to a rocky stream below, had no redeeming whitewash, no vines about their doors. The turf around them was worn away. Some were chimneyless; on others the thatch, where the weeds did not hold it together, had broken through, leaving great holes in the roof. On a bench, tilted up against the wall of the lowest of these cottages, sat an old gray-haired man in Tam o' Shanter, his head bent low, his clasped hands falling between his knees. It was a picturesque place, and we camped out a while under an old cart near the road-side. Perhaps it would have been wise if, like Mr. Hamerton, we could have seen only the picturesqueness of the Highland clachan, only the color and sublimity of the huts, only the fine women who live within them. But how could we sit there and not see that the picturesqueness was that of misery, that whatever color and sublimity there might be—and to the sublimity, I must confess, we were blind—were but outward signs of poverty and squalor, and that the huts sheltered not only strong young women, but feeble old men like that pathetic figure with the clasped hands and bent head? We have seen the old age of the poor, when we thought it but a peaceful rest after the work of years. In English almshouses we have found it in our hearts to envy the old men and women their homes; but here despair and sadness seemed the portion of old age. I do not know why it was, but as we watched that gray-haired man, though there was a space of blue sky just above him, and the day was warm and the air sweet, it was of the winter he made us think; of the time soon to come when the cold winds would roar through the pass, and snow would lie on the hills, and he would shiver alone in the chimneyless cottage with its one tiny window. A few miles away, men in a fortnight throw away on their fishing more than these people can make in years. Scotch landlords rent their wild, uncultivated acres for fabulous sums, while villages like this grow desolate. If, when you are in the Highlands, you would still see them as they are in the stupid romance of Scott or in the sickly sentiment of Landseer, or as a mere pleasure-ground for tourists and sportsmen, you must get the people out of your mind, just as the laird gets them off his estate. Go everywhere, by stage and steamboat, and when you come to a clachan or to a lonely cottage, shut your eyes and pass on; else you must realize, as we did—and more strongly as we went farther—that this land, which holiday-makers have come to look upon as their own, is the saddest on God's earth.

Before we left the shade of the cart a little girl went by, and we asked her the name of the village.

"Kilchrennan," she said, with impossible gutturals, and then she spelled it for us.

It was a good sign, we thought; if Highland children to-day are taught to spell, Highland men and women to-morrow may learn to think, and when they learn to think, then, let the landlord remember, they will begin to act.

After Kilchrennan, the road crossed the moorland, Ben-Cruachan towering far to our right. At the foot of the one wooded hill-side in all this heather-clad moor we met with the only adventure of the morning; for it was here we espied in the road, in front of us, a black bull. It fixed its horrid eyes upon us; its horns seemed to stretch from one side of the way to the other. We cast in our minds whether to go forward or through the wood, but we thought it best to get the trees between us, and we fled up the mountain and never stopped until we had left it a goodly space behind; for indeed it was the dreadfullest bull that ever we saw.

We came to another wretched village down by Loch Etive. Here again in the sunshine was an old man. He was walking slowly and feebly up and down, and there was in his face a look as if hope had long gone from him. In England, scarce a town or village is without its charities; but in the Highlands, while deer and grouse are protected by law, men are chased from their

KILCHRENNAN.

homes,* the aged and infirm are left to shift for themselves. I think the misery of these villages is made to seem but the greater because of the large house which so often stands close by. We looked from the weary, silent old man and the row of tiny bare cottages, to a gay young girl and a young man in a kilt, who together strolled lazily towards the large house just showing through the trees.

When Mr. Hamerton wrote his "Painters' Camp in the Highlands" he suggested a new route from Oban to Ballachulish by steamer up Loch Etive, and then by coach through Glen Etive and Glencoe. This is now one of the regular excursions from Oban, and one of the finest, I think, in the Highlands. In the glens we met no fewer than five coaches, so that I suppose the excursion is fairly popular. I wonder that Mr. Hamerton had a thought for the amusement of tourists, who are to him odious, as it seems necessary they should be to all right-minded writers of travel. Now, he might find loch and glens less fine. For the rest

---

* I have left this sentence as it is, though Mr. William Black was good enough to attack us for making such a statement. If he has any knowledge whatever on the subject, he must know that it was not until after the trial in Edinburgh— a trial held a little less than a year ago, when these pages had been already set up in type for the MAGAZINE—that it was discovered that deer are not protected by law in the Highlands. Men, as I have shown further on, cannot now be chased without reason from their homes, fixity of tenure being the chief good accomplished by the Crofter's Act of 1886.

of that day, being tourists ourselves, we bore with all others patiently.

With Taynuilt we left behind even the sparse cultivation of the Highlands. From the boat we saw that the mountain-slopes were unbroken by road or path; there was scarce a house in sight. Through Glen Etive the road was very rough, the mountains were barren, and not a sheep or cow was on the lower grassy hill-sides. It was all a deer forest, the guard told us, and even the English tourists in the coach exclaimed against the waste of good ground. It is well to go first through Glen Etive. Bare as it seemed to us, it was green when compared to

GLENCOE,

where rocks lay on the road and in the stream and on the hill-sides. The mountains rose bare and precipitous from their very base, and trees and grass found no place to grow.

The guard gave us the story of the massacre, with additions and details of his own which I have forgotten. At the end of the drive he charged two shillings—for his trouble, I suppose. People write of the emotions roused by scenery and associations. I think it is afterwards, by reading up on the subject, that one becomes first conscious of them. However that may be, of one thing I am certain: we have rarely been more flippant than we were on that day. In Glen Etive J—— discovered that Highland streams, where clear brownish water flows over a bed of yellow, green, and red stones, look like rivers of Julienne soup. In the high moor at the head of the Glen we were chiefly concerned with a lunch of milk and scones for a shilling, and grumblings over Highland extortion.

LOCH LEVEN, FROM BALLACHULISH.

In Glencoe, guard and driver pointed out the old man of the mountain, who is here the Lord Chancellor, and Ossian's Cave, on high in the rocky wall, and stopped to show us the Queen's View. But we were more interested in two cyclers pushing their machines up the steepest, stoniest bit of road; in a man in a long black frock-coat and silk hat with crape band, who carried an alpenstock with an umbrella strapped to it, and strode solemnly up the pass; in a species of gypsy van near Glencoe Inn, in which, the guard explained, twelve people and a driver travelled for pleasure. A girl looking very pale and wrapped in shawls sat at the inn door. The party had stopped on her account, he said; the drive had made her ill—and no wonder, we thought.

The stony pass led to a pleasant green valley, from which the road set out over the Bridge of Glencoe for the shores of Loch Leven and

BALLACHULISH.

Almost at once it brought us to a field overlooking the loch, where, apparently for our benefit, sports were being held.

The droning of the pipes made quite a cheerful sound, the plaids of the men a bright picture; and when, two miles beyond, we found the hotel with its windows turned towards the loch, we made up our minds not to push on to Oban, but to stay and spend Sunday here.

And so we had a second and longer look at the sports. Young men vaulted with poles; others, in full costume, danced Highland flings and the sword dance. Two pipers took turns in piping.

OBAN.

One had tied gay green ribbons to his pipe, and he fairly danced himself as he kept time with his foot. And while we watched we heard but Gaelic spoken. We were in a foreign country.

The position of the hotel was the best thing about it. At dinner an irate clergyman and his daughter took fresh offence at every course, until, when it came to the rice-pudding, they could stand it no longer and left the table. We were less nice, and made a hearty meal; but we thought so poorly of it that the next day, which was Sunday, we found a lunch of bread and cheese and beer more to our taste. This we ate at the inn in Glencoe, in company with the clergyman and his daughter. They were still sore—why, I could not understand—about the pudding, and the clergyman was consoling himself with a glass of good whiskey.

The following day we came to

OBAN—

the most odious place in the Highlands, I have heard it called; the most beautiful place in the world, Mr. William Black thinks. When the west wind blows and the sun shines, there is nothing like it for color, he told J——. We had to take his word for it. We found an east wind blowing and gray mist hanging over town and bay, and we could not see the hills of Mull. When we walked out in the late afternoon, it seemed a town of hotels and photograph shops, into which excursion trains were forever emptying excursionists and never carrying them away again. Crowds were on the parapetless, unsafe embankment; the bay was covered with boats. In front of the largest hotels bands were playing, and one or two of the musicians went about, hat in hand, among the passers-by. Fancy Hassler at Cape May sending one of his men to beg for pennies! It was dull, for all the crowd. The show of gayety was as little successful as the attempt of a shivering cockney to look comfortable in his brand-new kilt.

Altogether, Oban did not seem in the least lovely until we could no longer see it. But as the twilight grew grayer and the tide went out, the great curve of the embankment was marked by a circle of lights on shore and by long waving lines of gold in the bay. At the pier, a steamer, just arrived, sent up heavy clouds of smoke, black in the gathering grayness. The boats one by one hung out their lights. Oban was at peace, though tourists still walked and bands still played.

It was gray and inexpressibly dreary the next day at noon, when we took the boat for Tobermory, in Mull. Through a Scotch mist we watched Oban and its picturesque castle out of sight; through a driving rain we looked forth on the heights of Morven and of Mull. Sometimes the clouds lightened, and for a minute the nearer hills came out dark and purple against a space of whitish shining mist; but for the most part they hung heavy and black over wastes of water and wastes of land. Sir Walter Scott says that the Sound of Mull is the most striking scene in the Hebrides; it would have been fair to add, when storms and mists give one a chance to see it. Pleasure parties sat up on deck, wrapped in mackintoshes and huddled under umbrellas. Our time was divided between getting wet and drying off downstairs. The excitement of the voyage was the stopping of the steamer, now in mid-stream in "Macleod of Dare" fashion, now at rain-soaked piers. Of all the heroes who should be thought of between these two lands of romance, only the most modern was suggested to us, probably because within a few weeks we had been re-reading Mr. Black's novel. But, just as in his pages, so in the Sound of Mull, little boats came out to meet the steamer. They lay in wait, tossing up and down on the rough waters and manned with Hamishes and Donalds. Into one stepped a real Macleod, his collie at his heels; into another, an elderly lady, who was greeted most respectfully by the Hamish, as he lifted into his boat trunks marked with the name of Fleeming Jenkin. This gave us something to talk about; when we had last seen the name it was in a publisher's announcement, which said that Mr. Stevenson was shortly to write a biographical notice of the *late* Fleeming Jenkin.

At the piers, groups of people, no better off for occupation than we, waited to see the passengers land. We all took unaccountable interest in this landing. At Salen there was an intense moment when, as the steamer started, a boy on shore discovered that he had forgotten his bag. At the next pier, where a party of three got off, as their baggage was carried after them, we even went the length of counting up to forty bags and bundles, three dogs, and two maids. We left them standing there, surrounded by their property, with the rain pouring in torrents and not a house in sight. This is the way you take your pleasure in the Hebrides. We were glad to see among the boxes a case of champagne. At the last moment, one of the men, from the edge of the pier, waved a brown paper parcel, and told the captain that another like it had been left aboard. I am afraid he had forgotten something else; thence to Tobermory the captain did but revile him.

TOBERMORY

is a commonplace town with a semicircle of well-to-do houses on the shores of a sheltered bay. At one end of the wooded heights that follow the curve of the town is a big hotel; at the other, Aros House, a brand-new castle, in among the trees. The harbor is shut in by a long, narrow island, bare and flat. It seemed a place of endless rain and mist. But when we thought the weather at its worst, the landlady called it pleasant, and suggested a two miles' walk to the light-house on the coast. Children played on the street as if the sun shone. We even saw fishing parties row out towards the Sound.

We had to stay in Tobermory two interminable days, for it was impossible at first to find a way out of it. Our idea was to walk along the north and then the west coast, and so to Ulva; but the landlady was of the opinion that there was no getting from Tobermory except by boat. Fishermen in the bar-room thought they had heard of a rough road around the coast, and knew that on it we should find no inn. The landlord, to make an end of our questions, declared that we must go to Iona by the boat due the next morning at eight. This seemed the only chance of escape unless we were to return to Oban.

In the mean time there was nothing to do, nothing to see. The hotel windows looked out on the gray, cheerless bay, dotted with yachts. Once we walked in the rain to the light-house, and back across the moors. The wind never stopped blowing a gale.

"If anybody wants to know what Mull's like in summer," said J——, in disgust, "all they've got to do is to go to a New Jersey pine barren when an equinoctial's on."

At our early breakfast the next morning, the landlord told us that it was dark outside the bay. It must have been wilder even than he thought. No boat for Iona came.

It was after this disappointment that J——, by chance, in the post-office, met the Procurator Fiscal, whatever he may be. We have good reason to be grateful to him. He mapped out a walking route to Salen, and thence to Loch-Na-Keal, at the northern end of which is the island of Ulva—the soft Ool-a-va which always leads the chorus of the islands in Mr. Black's tragedy, "Macleod of Dare."

We did not care to walk to Salen in the rain; we were not willing to spend another night in Tobermory. Therefore, that same afternoon, when the boat from Skye touched at the pier, we got on board. We believed in the roughness of the sea beyond the Sound when we saw tourists prostrate in the cabin, with eloquent indifference to looks. But it was short steaming to

SALEN,

where we faced wind and rain to walk about a quarter of a mile to the hotel.

Here, as Dr. Johnson said in Glenelg, "of the provisions, the negative catalogue was very copious." The landlady asked us what we should like for supper; she might have spared herself the trouble, since she had nothing to give us but ham and eggs. However, we found the outlook less depressing than at Tobermory. There was no commonplace little town in sight, but only bare rolling grounds stretching to a bay, and on the shores the ruins of a real old castle, of which Mr. Abbey once very unkindly made a drawing, so that J——, for his own sake, thought it best to let it alone. There was, moreover, something to read. Lying with the guide-books were the "Life of Dr. Norman Mcleod," "Castle Dangerous," and the "Life of the Prince Consort." J—— devoured them all three, and the next day regaled me with choice extracts concerning the domestic virtues of the royal family.

When we awoke, the clouds were breaking. Across the Sound of Mull they were low on the heights of Morven, but the hill-sides were green, streaked with sunshine. Above were long rifts of blue sky, and in the bay a little yacht rocked on glittering water. We ate more ham and eggs, and made ready to begin our tramp at once.

Neither maid nor landlord could tell us if there were inns on the road to Bunessan. In Mull a man knows but his own immediate neighborhood. In the hotels, the farthest explorations are to the bed-rooms; in the cottages the spirit of enterprise is less. The interior of the island is an unknown country. The adventurous traveller goes no farther inland than Tobermory on the east coast, or Bunessan on the west. The ordinary traveller never goes ashore at all, but in the boat from Oban makes the tour of Mull in a day. As a consequence, there is no direct communnication between the two sides of the island. It is strange that, though one of the largest of the Hebrides and within easiest reach of the main-land, Mull should be one of the least known and civilized. It is not even settled. People respect Dr. Johnson because in the days when steamboats were not, and roads at the best were few, he made a journey to the islands. But we cannot help thinking that if this respect is measured by hardships, we are far more worthy of it for having followed him to Mull a centnry later. Wherever he and Boswell went, guides and horses, or boats, as the case might be, were at their disposal; the doors of all the castles and large houses in the islands were thrown open to them. We were our own guides. It may be said that the steamboat was at our service, but it could not always take us to places we wished to see. If Dr. Johnson had to ride over moorland on a pony too small for him, he was sure that when evening came a Macquarry, a Maclean, or a Macleod would be eager to make him welcome. We walked on roads, it is true, but they were bad, and not only were we not wanted

COAST OF MULL.

at the castles, but we did not want to go to them since they are now mostly in ruins; there was chance, too, of our not coming to an inn at nightfall. The inns of Mull are few and far between. Besides, for all one knows, those mentioned in the guide-book may be closed. If others have been opened, there is no one to tell you of them.

However, we took the procurator's word for the inn at Ulva, and started out again with our knapsacks, which seemed but heavier on our backs after several days' rest. All morning we tramped dreary miles of moor and hill, with the wind in our faces, and by lochs with endless curves, around which we had to go, though we saw our journey's end just before us. While we followed the northern shore of Loch-Na-Keal, high Ben-More, with its head among the clouds, was behind us. In front was the Atlantic, with heavy showers passing over it, and now blotting out far Staffa and the long ridge of the Ross of Mull, an encircling shadow between the ocean and the headland of Gribun; and now sweeping across the loch and the near green island of Inch-Kenneth.

A large house, with wide lawn and green fields and well-clipped hedges, just at the head of Loch-Na-Keal, and one or two small new cottages shut in with flaming banks of fuchsias, showed what Mull might be if in the island men were held in as high account as rabbits and grouse. We saw the many white tails of the rabbits in among the ferns, and though they live only to be shot, on the whole we thought them better off than the solemn, silent men and women who trudged by us towards Salen, where it was market-day, for it is their fate to live only to starve and suffer. The one man who spoke to us during that long morning was a shepherd, with a soft gentle voice and foreign Scotch, whose sheep we frightened up the hill-side.

ULVA

lay so close to the shores of Mull as scarce to seem a separate island. But the waters of the narrow Sound were rough. The postman, who had just been ferried over, held the boat as we stepped into it from the slippery stones of the landing. As he waited, he said not a word. They keep silence, these people, under the yoke they have borne for generations. The ferryman was away, and the boy who had come in his place had hard work to row against wind and waves, and harder work to talk English. "I beg pardon," was his answer to every question we asked.

The little white inn was just opposite the landing, and we went to it at once, for it was late and we were hungry. We asked the landlady if she could give us some meat.

"Of course," she said — and her English was fairly good—she could give us tea and eggs.

"No, but meat," we repeated.

"Yes, of course," she said again; "tea and eggs."

And we kept on asking for meat, and she kept on promising us tea and eggs, and I know not how the discussion had ended, if on a sudden it had not occurred to us that for her the word had none other but its Scriptural meaning.

While she prepared lunch we sat on low rocks by the boats drawn up high and dry on the stony beach. At the southern end of the island was Ulva House, white through an opening in a pleasant wood, and surrounded by broad green pastures. Just in front of us, close to the inn, a handful of bare black cottages rose from the mud in among rocks and bowlders. No paths led to the doors; nothing green grew about the walls. Women with pinched, care-worn faces came and went, busy with household work, and they were silent as the people we had met on the road. Beyond was barrenness; not another tree, not another bit of pasture-land was in sight. And yet, before the people were brought unto desolation, almost all the island was green as the meadows about the laird's house; and so it could be again if men were but allowed to cultivate the ground. Where weeds and rushes and ferns now cover the hills and the level places were once fields of grain and grass. To-day only the laird's crops are still sowed and reaped. Once there could be heard the many voices of men and women and children at work or at play, where now the only sounds are the roaring of the waters and the crack of the rifle.* Of all the many townships that were scattered from one end of the island to the other, there remains but this miserable group of cottages. The people have been driven from the land they loved, and sent hither and thither, some across the narrow Sound, others far across the broad Atlantic.

The Highlands and the Hebrides are lands of romance. There is a legend for almost every step you take. But the cruelest of these are not so cruel as, and none have the pathos of, the tales of their own and their fathers' wrongs and wretchedness which the people tell to-day. The old stories of the battle-field, and of clan meeting clan in deadly duel, have given way to stories of the clearing of the land that the laird or the stranger might have his shooting and fishing, as well as his crops. At first the people could not understand it. The evicted in Ulva went to the laird, as they would have gone of old, and asked for a new home. And what was his answer? "I am not the father of your family." And then, when frightened women ran and hid themselves at his coming, he broke the kettles they left by the well, or tore into

---

* This also has been questioned. All we can say is that we both saw and heard men in Ulva shooting with rifles. What they were shooting at we did not go to see.

ROSS OF MULL, LOOKING TOWARDS IONA.

shreds the clothes bleaching on the heather. And as the people themselves have it, "in these and similar ways he succeeded too well in clearing the island of its once numerous inhabitants, scattering them over the face of the globe." There must have been cruelty indeed before the Western Islander, who once loved his chief better than his own life, could tell such tales as these, even in his hunger and despair.

I know it is pleasanter to read of bloodshed in the past than of hunger in the present. A lately published book on Ireland has been welcomed by critics, and I suppose by readers, because in it is no mention of evictions and crowbar brigades and horrors of which newspapers make good capital. I have never been in Ireland, and it may be that you can travel there and forget the people. But in the Hebrides the human silence and the desolate homes and the almost unbroken moorland would let us, as foreigners, think of nothing else. Since our return we have read Scott and Mr. Hamerton and Miss Gordon Cumming and the Duke of Argyll, and many others who have helped to make or mar the romance and history of the Highlands. But the true story of the Highlands as they are I think we learned for ourselves when we looked, as we did at Ulva, from the laird's mansion to the crofter's hovel. It is the story of the tyranny of the few, the slavery of the many, which can be learned still more fully from the reports of the Royal Commission, published by the English Government.

When we returned to the inn we had no thought but to get away at once, how, we hardly knew. The landlady suggested three plans. We could wait until the morrow, when the Gomestra men, as she, a native, called them, and not Gometra men, as Mr. Black has it, would row us out to meet the steamboat coming from Iona. How "Macleod of Dare" like this would have been! We could be ferried over the Sound, and walk back by Loch-Na-Keal, the way we had come, then around its southern shores, and so across to Loch Scridain, at the head of which was an inn. Or we could sail across Loch-Na-Keal, and thus cut off many miles of the distance that lay between us and our next resting-place. We must, however, decide at once; there were two gentlemen below who would take us in their boat, but if we did not want them, they must go back to cut the laird's hay. Were we willing to wait until evening, they would take us for half price. The rain now fell on the loch, but we made our bargain with the gentlemen on the spot.

The landlady gave our sailing quite the air of an adventure. We need not be alarmed, she said, as indeed we had not thought of being; the only danger was to the gentlemen coming home. We found them at the landing, ballasting the boat with stones and getting on their oil-skins. We suggested that they should take us all the way to Bunessan, but they would not hear of it. Only the older of the two, an old gray-haired man, could speak English; they would not venture out to sea in such weather, he told us.

As we sailed past the white house we asked him if he had ever heard of Dr. Johnson. He shook his head and then turned to the other man, and the two began to talk in Gaelic. "Toctor Shonson, Toctor Shonson," we heard them say to each other. But they both kept shaking their heads, and finally the old man again said they had never heard of him.

When the wind swept the rain from the hills of Ulva, we could see that on the western side of the island the strange basaltic formation like that of Staffa begins. Near the low green shores of Inch-Kenneth a yacht lay at anchor. It belonged to one of the lairds of Mull, the boatman said. The people, who have barely enough to live on themselves, can still afford to support a yacht for their landlord. How this can be is the real problem of the Hebrides. To solve it is to explain the crofter question without the aid of a Royal Commission.

On the Gribun shore the landing-place was a long row of stones, slippery with wet sea-weed.

The old man gave me his arm and led me in safety to the foot of the meadows beyond. He was the gentleman the landlady had called him. A Frenchman could not have been more polite. Nor was there in his politeness the servility, which in England makes one look to honest rudeness with relief. Caste distinctions may be bitterly felt in the homes of the Western Islanders, but in their manner is something of the equality which French republicans love. They can be courteous without cringing. Englishmen call this familiarity. But then the Englishman who understands true politeness is the exception.

It was, if anything, wetter on land than it had been on the water. To reach the road we waded through a broad meadow knee-high in dripping grass. The mist kept rising and falling, and one minute we could see the islands—Ulva and Gometra and Inch-Kenneth and even Staffa—and the next only grayness. In the narrow pass over the headland between Loch-Na-Keal and Loch Scridain the clouds rolled slowly down the mountains on either side, lower and lower, until presently we were walking through them. And as we went, as was proper in the land of Macleod of Dare, a strange thing happened; for scarcely had the clouds closed about us than a great gust of wind swept through the pass and whirled them away for a moment. Then the wind fell, and again we were

HEADLAND OF GRIBUN, FROM ULVA.

swallowed up in grayness, and could scarcely see. Just as we were within sight of Loch Scridain, down poured torrents of rain. A little farther on and we were half-way up to our knees in a bridgeless stream that came rushing down the mountains across the road.

We passed two wind-and-rain-beaten villages and occasional lonely cottages, and the ruins of others. Mr. Hamerton says that nothing is more lovely to an artist than a Highland cottage after a rain; but the trouble is, you seldom see it after the rain, for in the Hebrides the rain it raineth every day and always. We came, too, to one big dreary house and a drearier kirk. The rest of the way there was but the wet wilderness, with the wet road following the curves of the loch, and even striking a mile or so inland to cross with the bridge a river which falls into it at its head. The inn was on the opposite shore; a short-cut lay across the water; there were boats moored to the northern bank where we walked, but not a ferryman to be found. A woman in a clean white cap, who stood in a cottage door-way, did not even know if there was a ferry.

Towards evening the rain stopped; the light of the setting sun shone on the hills before us as it seldom does except in pictures of the Hebrides; but on a walking tour when the chance for pleasure comes, one's capacity for enjoyment has gone.

At the end of a day's tramp one can see little beauty, save that of a good dinner and a soft bed, both of which are the exception in the Hebrides.

The inn at
KINLOCH
was a two-storied cottage, with kitchen full of women and tap-room full of geese and hens below stairs, dining and sleeping rooms above. The bed-rooms were all occupied—by the family, I suppose, since we were given our choice; but after choosing, everything had to be moved out before we could move in. However, we made a shift to change our shoes and stockings, and in the dining-room we crouched over a big fire, while the steam rose in clouds from our soaked tweeds. The land-lady came up at once with whiskey and glasses.

"And will you accept a glass from me?" she asked.

This was the Highland hospitality of which one reads, and it was more to our taste than the whiskey.

For supper of course we had ham and eggs, but it took no less than two hours for the landlady to cook them and to set the table. She was the sister of the landlady at Ulva, she told us. "And it's a good house my sister keeps whatever," she said; and then she wanted to know, "Had the wee laddie, Donald, ferried us over? And we had come from Salen, and were we going to Bunessan? It will be twelve miles to Bunessan whatever. And then to Iona?" It will be a great kirk we should see there, she had heard; but she had never been to Iona. She spoke excellent English, with the soft, drawling accent we thought so pleasant to hear, and we wished she could cook as well as she talked.

While we waited, J——, out of sympathy, fed a lean hound on meat-lozenges. He looked so starved that we could but hope each would prove for him the substantial meal it is said to be on the label of the box, and which we had not yet found it.

After supper it was two hours more before the bedroom was ready, and I think we had rarely been so tired. We sat nodding over the fire, sick with sleep. When we could stand it no longer, we made a raid upon the room while the landlady, who spent most of her time on the stairs, was on her hundredth pilgrimage below, and locked ourselves in. After that, she kept coming back with towels and one thing and another until we were in bed and asleep.

We had ordered more ham and eggs for eight o'clock in the morning, and asked to be awakened at seven. We might have spared ourselves the trouble—no one called us. It was half-past nine before breakfast was on the table, and it would not have been served then had not J—— gone into the kitchen to see it cooked. The only difference between our morning and evening meal was in the bill, where, according to island reckoning, tea and ham and eggs called supper, are worth sixpence more than eggs and ham and tea called breakfast.

At the last moment up came the landlady, again with whiskey and glasses.

"And will you accept a glass from me?"

But indeed we could not. To begin a twelve miles' walk with whiskey was out of the question. We afterwards learned that this was but good form on her part. The true Highlander always expects to drink a wee drappie with the coming and the parting guest. It would have been true politeness for us to accept. However, we did not know it at the time, and the whiskey was bad. She seemed hurt by our refusal. I thought her a shade less cordial when we came to say goodby.

The wind was still blowing a gale, but it drove the clouds beyond the bald mountains towards Ben-More, and brought no showers with it. Everything had grown bright with the morning but the cottages, and they, perhaps because of the contrast with the blue loveliness of water and sky and hills, seemed darker and more desolate than in the rain. Here and there along the loch a few were gathered in melancholy groups, pathless and chimneyless, smoke pouring from door-ways and through holes in the walls, mud at the very thresholds. For every cottage standing there was another in ruins. On the top of a low hill, over which we made a short-cut, was a deserted village, conveniently out of sight of the road. No traveller, unless he chanced upon it as we did, would know of it. It was not high enough or far enough from other cottages for the shielings upon which the Duke of Argyll thinks so much false sentiment has been wasted. We found a few blackfaced sheep in possession of the ruins, and before them, I fear, have been driven not merely cattle from summer pastures, but men from their only homes. There were several school-houses between Kinloch and Bunessan, and we half hoped that these were in a measure responsible for roofless walls and desolate hearths. But the truth is, the Duke of Argyll and other landlords of Mull find it less trouble to collect rents from a few large tenants than from many small ones, and to suit their convenience the people have had to go. It is their land; why should they not do with it as they think best?

Almost all this Ross of Mull, on which we now were, belongs to the Duke of Argyll, the defender of Scotland as it was and as it is; and I think in all the Hebrides there is no place more desolate. We saw perhaps more signs of bitter poverty in Skye and in Barra. But in these islands the evicted have settled again upon the crofts of their friends or relations. Often it is because the many are thus forced to live upon land that can scarce support the few that all are so poor. But the Islander loves his home as he once loved his chief, and now hates his landlord, and he must be in extremity indeed before he will go from it. Knowing this, you feel the greatness of the misery in the Ross of Mull, from which the people have flown as if from a plague-stricken land. The greater part of it is silent and barren as the desert. We walked for miles, seeing no living things save a mere handful of sheep grazing on the hills, and the white sea-gulls perched on the low sea-weed covered rocks of Loch Scridain. And beyond the barren waste of land was the sea without a sail upon its waters, and the lonely islands, which we knew were no less desolate. The cruel climate of this far northern country has had little to do with the people's flight. Neither, indeed, has natural barrenness. The soil in the Highlands is not naturally barren, the Duke of Argyll himself has said. The few large farms by the way were good proof of what might be, even in the rocky Ross of Mull.

It seemed odd in the midst of the wilderness to meet two peddlers loaded with gay gilt frames. They thought it a "blowy" day, and so did a man who passed soon after in a dog-cart. But the women in clean white caps whom we met on the road could answer our questions only in streams of Gaelic.

We saw no one else but men and women getting in the harvest, or bending beneath great burdens of sea-weed as they toiled up the hill from the shores of the loch. There was a lonely graveyard by the way; but nowhere does death seem so great a blessing as we thought it must be here.

It was a long twelve miles, and the knapsacks were growing heavier with each day. But we were walking for our lunch; there were no inns on our road. For one reason or another, to me it was our hardest day's work. I think I must have starved had not J—— slung my knapsack on his already heavily laden shoulders. At the last,

BUNESSAN

came as a surprise. We were looking sadly at the endless line of road over the moors in front of us, when we turned a corner, and there was the little white town, with a pleasant inn, close to the waters of Loch Slach.

We had to wait—we were growing used to waiting—for our lunch; but at last when it came it seemed a banquet. We were not asked to eat either ham or eggs. Altogether, we were so well pleased that we brought the day's walk to an end. But it seemed that the maid who came to the door was less pleased with us. Our knapsacks, too large for comfort, were too small for respectability. Our clothes were weather-worn. The landlord bade her show us to a bedroom; but before we had finished our lunch she had locked every door in the house, carefully leaving the keys on the outer side, and, in her zeal, locking one man in. This, however, we did not learn until later, when English people staying in the inn told us what suspicious characters we were. They said she was stupid, which we had already found out for ourselves.

Bunessan is the show-place of the Ross of Mull; steamers occasionally land at a pier on the loch, two miles distant. Tourists come to the inn for the fishing. If they go no farther into the island, they probably carry away with them impressions of well-to-do people and benevolent landlords—the impressions, probably, the Duke of Argyll wishes to produce. After Kilpatrick and the other wretched groups of cottages we had passed in the morning, it did indeed seem happy and prosperous. It may be that we should have been less struck with it and its inn had it not been for the things we had already seen and experienced. Certainly, at dinner, dishes which we thought luxuries were found fault with by the rest of the company. But then they had their own opinion of Bunessan. They had taken it on trust, after hearing it praised; but no sooner had they come than they wished themselves away again.

One suggested that friends should be induced to stay for a summer and educate the place, which might thus be made bearable for them in the future; but the others would not hear of it—one trial was quite enough. We were all very confidential about our plans, and took pleasure in mutually discouraging each other. J—— and I were foolish, they said, to go to Iona, where the cathedral was so insignificant that from the steamer they mistook it for the parish church. We, on our side, declared it worse than folly for them to go from Bunessan to Tobermory, the dreariest spot in all the dreariness of Mull. In the end we agreed that our coming to the island was a mistake, and that no one but Mr. Black could have a good word to say for it. Somehow, we made it seem—and it was a comfort to find some one else to abuse—as if he had brought us here under false pretences. But, indeed, whoever thinks to find Mull as it is described in "Macleod of Dare" cannot but be disappointed. Castle Dare must have been not very far from Bunessan, on the Ross of Mull. It was to this very inn Lady Macleod wished to send Gertrude White and her father; and when you have seen the home of the Macleods for yourself, you would have, like Mr. Black, no mercy for Sir Keith, but you would spare his sweetheart.

The fact is, Mr. Black's descriptions are misleading, though I must admit that even as we found fault with him, one of his strange things happened; for, far out beyond the loch and its purple hills we saw Staffa, and the sea below and the sky above it, turned to gold as the sun sank into the Atlantic. But then, as a rule, the things that happen in Mull are less strange than disagreeable. For one evening's loveliness, you must put up with hours of cold and damp discomfort. Of course, if you own a castle or a yacht, you can improve your point of view.

In the morning after this beautiful sunset, the wind blew the rain through the window in gusts over our toilet-table. Again no one called us. The morning hours of the Hebrides are even later than those of London, which we had hitherto supposed the latest in the working world. When we went down-stairs there were cups and saucers and plates on the breakfast-table, but nothing else; when we asked for our bill the maid said we should have it in a wee bittee, which we knew to mean long hours, and J——, as at Kinloch, took matters into his own hands.

For the first time we felt our superiority as we shouldered our knapsacks. Because of the early rain and wind, the other people in the inn had given up the boat to Tobermory. Already, breakfast over, the rain stopped and clouds grew light. We were on our way to Iona while they still made plans to follow us with their babies and bundles.

"ONE OF HIS STRANGE THINGS HAPPENED."

The road lay for six miles over the moors. There were two or three large houses with cultivated fields, a few black dreary cottages, and the ruins of others. But this end of the Ross of Mull was mostly, as when David Balfour walked across it, bog and brier and big stones. The coast was all rock, great piles of red granite jutting out in uneven masses into the sound that separates Iona from the Ross. When we reached it the ferryman had just come and gone. It was the 11th of August, and men with guns, in readiness for the morrow, were getting into a dog-cart, its horses' heads turned towards Bunessan. Two fishermen, in a boat filled with lobster nets, rowed to the tiny landing. We asked them to take us across, but with a word they refused. There was nothing to do but to sit on the rocks and wait, in fear lest the party from Bunessan, with their children and endless boxes and bundles—thirteen, one man told us he had—should overtake us and give us and our knapsacks no chance in the inns of Iona.

Wind and rain blew in our faces. The fishermen made off in their little boat, hugging the rocky shore. Above us, on the granite, were two cottages, no less naked and cold. Across the Sound we looked to a little white town low on the wind-swept water, and to a towered cathedral dark against the gray-green rocks. A steamer had just brought Cook's daily pilgrims to St. Columba's shrine.

ON THE ISLANDS.

ALL things come to those who wait, even the ferry-men of the Hebrides; but the steamer had carried the pilgrims far from St. Columba's Island towards Staffa before the little ferry-boat sailed with the wind, round the rocks, into the tiny bay by the landing. One passenger was put out, and a woman ran down from the black cottages for a bundle done up in a handkerchief, from which, as she took it, fell out broken pieces of bread and meat. Unconsciously, these people are always reminding you of their poverty.

There was no sailing in the teeth of the wind. The ferry-man and a small boy with him rowed, keeping under the shelter of the rocks as far as possible. At first both were silent. But we were fast learning that this silence is not the stupidity or surliness which the stranger in the islands is apt to think it. It comes rather of the sadness which has been the Western Islander's inheritance for generations, and of his shyness in speaking the foreign Scotch — that is, if he can speak it at all — for which he is so often laughed at. Once you break through the silence, and show the people that you do not look upon them as children or as slaves, they are friendly enough.

All this part of the Ross of Mull, as far as we could see, belonged to the Duke of Argyll, our ferry-man said. There had been trouble here as in Tiree, and the Commission was coming in a week. He had only his house and his boat. Five shillings and sixpence a year he paid; it was not much, but it was about the land there was trouble, and he had no land. We might have agreed with him and thought his rent no great thing, had we not seen his bare cottage, stranded on the bare rocks, probably built by himself or by his father before him. As it was, it seemed to us, if there was any question of payment, it should have been the other way.

Our stay in Iona was the one perfect part of our journey. In the first place, we were free to wander where and how we chose without thought of long miles to be walked before nightfall, and, better still, without our knapsacks, which we left in the inn. It was no small surprise to learn that we had our choice of three hotels. After careful study of "Macleod of Dare," we rather expected to be stranded on an almost uninhabited island. We can now recommend Mr. Black, on his next visit, to try the very excellent house at which we stayed. This was St. Columba's Inn. We went to it, not so much to do honor to the saint as because it was the biggest in the place, the nearest to the cathedral, and commanded the finest view.

Southward, it looked to the broken walls of the nunnery rising high above house roofs and chimneys, and farther to a sweep of water, and farther

IN THE TRANSEPT OF THE CATHEDRAL, IONA.

still to the Ross of Mull, the low black rock of Erraid, the isle Mr. Stevenson has made famous, at its far end. In the distance, shadowy islands lay over the gray sea. To the north was the cathedral and the ruined monastery.

The inn was quite full, but the landlady promised us a room in the manse, a short way down the road.

Iona is the show-place by which we fancied the Duke of Argyll must hope to answer the question, once in a great while asked, about misery, terrorism, extortion, rent, in the Hebrides. Strangers come to the islands only to fish or to shoot. It is the exception when, as at Iona, there are sights to be seen. They have time to give only a glance to the Islander and his home. In Iona this home seems decent enough; if you stop to ask the Islander what he thinks, however, I doubt if it will be praise alone you will hear of his model landlord. Above the stony beach, where boats lie among the rocks, is the village street, lined with white cottages; and beyond, fields of tall grain and good pasture slope upward to the foot of the low green hills, whose highest peak rises to the north of the village, a background for the cathedral. Many of the cottages are new, others are whitewashed into comparative cheerfulness. The crops on the lower ground, the sheep and cattle on the hills, are pleasanter to see in an island where men live than endless wastes of heather. In Iona the civilization of the monks of the Dark Ages has survived even the modern sportsman.

It is the fashion among writers of guide and other books about Iona to call it a desolate, lonely little isle. That it is little I admit; but you must

go to the other side of the Sound for the loneliness and desolation. In proportion to its size, it seemed to us the most cultivated island of the Hebrides. I have heard it argued that for the Duke of Argyll not to forfeit his ownership was a true charity to his tenants, as if Iona was still the desert St. Columba found it. But I think its rental would be found a fair return for the charity of a landlord. As for the favorite myth that Iona is far out in the Hebridean Sea, I hardly know how it could have arisen, since the island is within easy reach of the main-land and of Mull. There is no history of its old monastery that does not tell how the pilgrim coming to it from the Ross of Mull had but to call a summons from the granite rocks, and the monks would hear the cry and make ready to meet him in their boats. If this be true, however, his voice must have been phenomenal. The modern pilgrim could no more do this than he could wield the long sword or pull the cross-bow of men of old. In our time a steamer comes to Iona every day from Oban, and twice a week another stops on its way to and from Glasgow and the Outer Hebrides. If Iona lay so near American shores it would long since have become a Bar Harbor or a Campo Bello. Even where it is it has its crowds of visitors. The writer who on one page tells you of its loneliness, on the next mourns its daily desecration when tourists eat sandwiches among the ruins.

These ruins, like everything else in Iona, belong to the Duke of Argyll. They are kept locked except when the keeper of the keys opens them to sight-seers. It may interest his Grace to know that we trespassed, climbing over the low stone

TOMB OF MACLEOD.

walls into the cathedral enclosure. While we were there we were alone, save for black sheep, the modern successors of the monks. It is a fact that as we stood with our feet upon Macleod of Macleod's tomb, one of the black sheep—probably the very same which frightened Gertrude White in the moonlight — baaed at us. But the sun was shining, and we did not screech; we merely said *shoo* to it, and remarked upon its impudence.

If our piety, with Dr. Johnson's, did not grow warmer among the ruins of Iona, at least our way of seeing them was not unlike Boswell's. Perhaps this is why we think he showed more common-sense in Iona than elsewhere on his journey. He did not trouble to investigate minutely, he says, "but only to receive the general impression of solemn antiquity, and the particular ideas of such objects as should of themselves strike my attention." But indeed, unless you have a lifetime to spend in Iona, unless you are an architect or an archæologist, there is little need to care where the exact site of infirmary or refectory or library may be, or to whom this shrine was set up, that tombstone laid, or in what year walls were built, windows opened. It is enough to see how beautiful the monks could make the holy place they loved, here on this rough northern coast, as in among the vineyards and olives of the south, as in English fenland and wooded valley.

But if Boswell's impression was one of disappointment, ours was one of wonder to find the ruins so much more perfect than we had expected, and so beautiful, not only with the beauty of impressiveness as a whole, but with a grace and refinement of detail one does not look for in the far north.

Much early Italian work is not more graceful than the carving on the capitals, the tracery in the windows, the door-way leading into the sacristy, the arches that spring from the cloister walls to their outer arcade in the monastery and church founded by St. Columba. If, as has been said, no ivy covers the walls, when we were there yellow flowers had pushed their way between the stones, while windows and rounded arches made a framework for the unbroken blue of sea and sky and pale distant hills. For so long as we were in the cathedral, the sun shone as if, instead of Hebridean seas, the Mediterranean lay beyond. True, this did not last half a morning; it rained before night; but the very breaks in the sunshine, and the way the clouds came and went, made the day more beautiful.

It is strange to see this wonderful work of other days in an island where, owing to their present masters, men can now scarce support existence. Centuries of progress or deterioration—which is it?—lie between the cathedral, lovely even in ruin, and the new ugly kirk close by. And yet when men had time to make their world beautiful the harvest was as rich. There was enough to eat and to spare for the stranger when the Celtic knots and twists were first carved on the cross standing by the cathedral door and looking seaward, and on the tombs lying within the chancel.

But, and more's the pity, the same cannot be said to-day, when tombs are crumbling, and pale green lichens cover the carving of the cross. You feel this contrast between past and present still more in the graveyard by St. Oran's chapel, into which also we made our way over a stone wall. The long grass has been cleared from the gray slabs, where lie the mitred bishops and the men in armor, or where the intricacy of the Celtic designs makes space for a ship with its sails spread. They are "only gravestones flat on the earth," as Boswell says, and now neatly placed in senseless rows for the benefit of the tourist. But who would exchange them for the well-polished granite obelisks of the modern stone-cutter which rise at their side?

The old road leads from the cathedral, past McLean's weather-worn cross — which is so thin you wonder that it still withstands the strong winds from the sea—to the nuns' convent, whose ruins and tombs show it to have been only less fine than the monastery. Here the gate was thrown open. A small steam-yacht, which we could see lying at anchor in the Sound below, had just let loose a dozen yachtsmen upon the loneliness of Iona, and they were being personally conducted through the nunnery.

We trespassed no more, except in fields on the western side of the island, whither we walked by the very road, for all I know, along which St. Columba was carried in the hour before death, that he might once more see the monks working on the land he had reclaimed, and there give them his last blessing. But if we trespassed, no one objected. The men whom we met greeted us in Gaelic, which, when they saw we did not understand, they translated into a pleasant good-day or directions about our path.

There were many other places we should have seen. But since the whole island was a proof of St. Columba's wisdom in settling on it, nothing was to be gained by a visit to the particular spot where he landed or where he set up a cairn. And as for the Spouting Cave, we took the guide-book's word for it; for as Dr. Johnson would say, we were never much elevated by the expectation of any cave. Instead of sight-seeing, we stayed on the western shore, looking out beyond the low white and grass-grown sand-dunes and the bowlder-made beach to the sea, with its many rocky isles, the fear of seamen, black upon the waters. It is just such a coast as Mr. Stevenson has described in his "Merry Men." And, indeed, since I have written this I have read in his "Memoirs of an Islet" that it is this very coast, though more to the south of Iona, where the *Christ-anna* and the *Covenant* went down to the bottom, there to rot with the *Espirito Santo* and her share of the treasures of the Invincible Armada. When Columba sailed from Ireland to Hebridean seas the Merry Men had long since begun their bonny dance, for they are as old as the rocks against which they dash, and these rocks are older than man. When you know the dangers of this coast you have no little respect for the saint who dared them. St. Columba and his disciples, who set up cross and bell on lonely St. Kilda and the far Färöe Islands, were the Stanleys and Burtons of their time.

People who have never heard of crofters and their troubles can tell you all about St. Columba and his miracles. In Iona he interested us chiefly because all that is left of his and his followers' work gives the lie to modern landlords. Land in the Hebrides, they say, is only fit for deer and grouse. St. Columba showed that it could be made fit for man as well.

The landlady of St. Columba's Inn is true to the traditions of the island. She is as unwilling to turn the stranger from her door as were the abbots of St. Columba's monastery. In her own way she performs miracles and finds room for every one who comes. At first we thought that her miracles were worked at our expense. During our absence the party from Bunessan had arrived. Although their boxes were on the rocks of the Ross of Mull, awaiting the ferry-man's convenience, by their very numbers they had gained the advantage we feared, and had quietly stepped into the room in the manse, of which we had neglected to take possession. We were now quartered in the schoolhouse. However, to judge from our comfort there, we lost nothing by the change.

It was at the late supper that we enjoyed the "dairy produce" of which Miss Gordon Cumming writes with rapture. It was a simple meal, such as one might have shared with St. Columba himself. The breakfasts and dinners, I should add, were less saintly, and therefore more substantial. As for the rest of the island, the fare is regulated by poverty and the Duke. We make a great to-do at home over the prohibition question, but in the Highlands they manage these matters more easily. Ducal option, we were told, reigns throughout the island. And yet the people of Iona are not grateful for thus being spared the trouble of deciding for themselves upon a subject whereon so few men agree. It has been whispered that drunkenness is not unknown in the Blessed Isle, and that natives have been seen by strangers—oh, the scandal of it!—reeling under the very shadow of the cathedral.

A white-haired clergyman, with pleasant old-fashioned manners and Gladstone collar, presided at supper. He introduced us at once to his family. "My son"—and he waved his hand towards a youth we had seen crossing the fields with his color-box—" my son is an artist; he is studying in the Royal Academy. He has already sold a picture for forty pounds. Not a bad beginning, is it? And my daughter," and he lowered his voice deferentially, "will soon be in the hands of the critics. She has just made some wonderfully clever illustrations for an old poem that hit her fancy!"

It was pleasant to see his fatherly pride. For his sake we could have wished her in an easier position.

Evidently, when you have exhausted saintly gossip in Iona you are at the end of your resources. The clergyman and two or three others with him were as eager to hear where we had been and where we were going and what we had seen, as if they had had nothing to talk about for a fortnight. We had decided to take the *Dunara Castle* from Glasgow, and in it to steam to Coll and Tiree and the Long Island. We had heard of the steamer, as you hear of everything in the Hebrides, by chance. And now the old man was all for having us change our minds. Here we were, safe in Iona, he said; why should we brave the dangers of the wild coast? Another man thought we had better not go to Harris; he had arrived there one Saturday evening, intending to remain two weeks; but the midges would give him no peace, and he had left with the steamer on Monday morning. The only comfort he could give was that they would feed us well on the *Dunara Castle*. It is strange that in Scotland, no matter what your plans may be, your fellow-tourists are sure to fall foul of them.

It was after this the clergyman brought out of his pocket a handful of the new coins, which we had not then seen.

"It's an ugly face," said J——, thinking only of the coin, though it would have been no libel had he referred to her gracious Majesty herself.

But the clergyman was down upon him at once. "I cannot let any one speak disrespectfully of my queen in my presence," he cried; "I love her too dearly to hear a word against her."

And he told us how, that afternoon, he had climbed to the top of the highest hill in Iona; and standing where Columba had stood so many hundreds of years ago, and remembering that this was the Jubilee year of his beloved sovereign, he dropped a new shilling into the cairn which marks the spot where the monks first made their home.

And yet I have a friend who, in the pages of the *Atlantic Monthly*, has tried to prove that sentiment is fast decaying.

Later, when this same sentimentalist told us of the poverty, hunger, and misery in Iona, we thought that the shilling might have been dropped to better purpose.

It was on a gray morning that an old Hamish rowed us and two other passengers and a load of freight to the "DUNARA CASTLE," which had dropped anchor in the middle of the Sound. On deck we found four young sportsmen in knickerbockers and ulsters, their backs turned upon the cathedral, firing at sea-gulls and missing them very successfully. In fact, I might as well say here, they kept on firing and missing so long as they were on the steamer. A man with a wife, four children, three maids, and a deckful of baggage, was already preparing to get off at Bunessan. The domestic energy of the Englishman is only less admirable than his business-like methods of pleasure. A party of Lowlanders were playing cards. A man of universal authority was telling a small group of listeners all about the geology and religion, the fishing and agriculture, of the islands. But as we sat in a corner, sheltered from the bitter cold wind, the talk that came to us was mostly of sport.

"I played that brute for half an hour!"

"I was fishing with a worm, I think."

"The best thing for shooting rooks is an air-gun."

"He wasn't a particularly good shot."

And all the time the brave sportsmen kept showing us what particularly bad shots they were.

Is Tartarin's *Chasse de Casquettes* really so much funnier than what is called sport in England?

Suddenly one of the Scotchmen, leaving his cards to look about him, gave the talk an unexpected literary turn. "That feller, Louis Stevverson," he said, "laid one o' the scenes o' his Keednopped here," and he pointed to the Ross and Errald.

"Woo's 'e?" said a cockney.

"'Arts is trumps," announced a third, and literature was dropped for more engrossing themes.

Emerson was right. It would be a waste of time for the literary man to play the swell. Even the handsome and gentlemanly authors of Boston, who are praised by Arlo Bates, when they become known to the world at large may be but "fellers!"

From the Sound we steamed past the great headland of Gribun, with the caves in its dark rocks, and into Loch Slach to the pier near Bunessan. The sportsmen were the first to alight, and, with guns over their shoulders, they disappeared quickly up the hill-side. The father of the family, like a modern Noah, stood on the pier to count his wife, children, maid, boxes, bundles, fishing-rods, and gun-cases, and to see them safely on dry land. It was fortunate for the original Noah that he did not have a whole ship's company to fee when he left the Ark. We were some time putting off and taking on freight. At the last moment, back ran the four sportsmen, bearing one bird in triumph. They parted with it sadly and tenderly. It was pathetic to see their regret after they had given it to a fisherman, who seemed embarrassed by the gift. I think they knew that it was the last bird they would bring down that day.

Then again we steamed past Gribun. Beyond it rose Inch-Kenneth and Ulva, really "Ulva dark" this morning. And one by one we left behind us, Iona, its white sands shining, its cathedral standing out boldly against the sky; Staffa, for a time so near that we could see the entrance to the great cave with its clustered piers; Fladda, Lunga, and the Dutchman's Cap. It was a page from "Macleod of Dare." And what were the Dhu Harteach men saying now? we could not help asking. Everywhere we looked were tiny nameless islands and bits of rock, sometimes separated only by a narrow channel. And now the sun shone upon us in our corner and made us warm. And even after the hills of Mull had begun to go down on the horizon, and Iona and Staffa had faded into vague shadows, we could see the Dutchman, like a great Phrygian cap set upon the waters.

Straight out we went to Tiree, a long, treeless strip of land with low hills at one end, and a wide, sandy, Jersey-like beach. A few houses, scattered here and there, were in sight. There was no pier.

A large boat, with three men at each of the four long oars, came out to meet the steamer, and into it were tumbled pell-mell men and women, and tables, and bags of meal, and loaves of bread, and boxes. It is another of the Duke of Argyll's islands. Looking at it from the steamship point of view, one could not but wonder if as much good might not be done for people, whose only highway is the ocean, by the building of a pier as by prohibition laws enforced by a landlord. As in Iona, so in Tiree, no spirits can be bought or sold. It is one of the anomalies of paternal government that the men made children turn upon their kind fatherly ruler. The crofters of Tiree have given trouble even as have those of Skye and Lewis. They are shielded from drunkenness, and yet they complain that they have been turned from the land that once was theirs to cultivate, and that their rents have been for long years so high that to pay them meant starvation for their families. Though these complaints are explained by the Duke as "phenomena of suggestion" to the Commissioners, part at least seemed well founded on fact. Instead of £1251 18s. according to his own estimate, his Grace, according to that of the Commission, is now entitled to but £922 10s. from the island of Tiree.

We had not time to land, but steaming past its miserable shores, it seemed dreary enough. St.

CASTLE BAY, FROM BARRA.

Columba showed what he thought of it when he sent penitents there to test their sincerity. The island of Coll, to which Dr. Johnson and Boswell were carried in a storm, was as flat and stupid and dreary. We had come as far as Coll, partly because of the Doctor's visit. But from this time until we left the Hebrides we were so much taken up with what we saw as scarce to give him another thought. For a while we went many miles astray from his route.

When you steam from Tiree and Coll, a broad stretch of the Atlantic lies between you and the Long Island. If I had my choice, I would rather cross the Channel from Newhaven to Dieppe, and that is saying the worst that can be said. The sunshine for the day came to an end. It was cruelly cold. The sportsmen fell prone upon the deck, and the intervals between their now languid shots were long. The man of authority shut himself up in his state-room, the best on the steamer. The card-players sat sad and silent. We, for our part, could only think of our folly in coming, and wonder if we too must be sick. Surely walking could not be greater misery than this. Though in these seas you are never quite out of sight of land, and never clear of the big and little rocks cropping up all around you, it was not until late in the afternoon that we came again close to large islands. They were wild and desolate, with hardly a house and but few cattle and sheep on their rocky shores. One or two boats, with brown sails raised, were jumping and pitching over the waves.

The gray wretchedness of the afternoon was a fit prelude to Barra. When we came to Castle Bay, rain was falling upon its waters, on the battlemented castle perched upon a rocky, sea-weed-covered islet, and on the town, set against a background of high bare hills. But the steamer stopped, and we went ashore to look about us. A few ugly new houses, shops with plate-glass windows, often cited as proofs of the island's prosperity, and then the real Barra: a group of black cottages—compared to which those of Mull were mansions, those of Kilchrennan palaces—running up and down the rocky hill-side. Only by a polite figure of speech can the stone pile in which the Hebridean crofter makes his home be called a cottage. It is, as it was described many years ago, but "a heavy thatched roof thrown over a few rudely put together stones." The long low walls are built of loose stones blackened by constant rain. The thatched roof, almost as black, is held in place without by a net-work of ropes, within by rafters of drift-wood. The crofter has no wood save that which the sea yields, and yet in some districts he must pay for picking up the beams and spars washed up on his wild shores, just as he must for the grass and heather he cuts from the wilder moorland when he makes his roof. Not until you come close to the rough stone heap can you see that it is a house, with an opening for door-way, one tiny hole for window. From a distance there is but its smoke to distinguish it from the rocks strewn around it.

At Castle Bay, where many of these "scenes of misery," as Pennant called them one hundred years ago, were grouped together, there was not even the pretence of a street, but just the rock, rough, ragged, and broken, as God made it. The people who live here are almost all fishermen, and, as if in token of their calling, they have fashioned the thatch of their roofs into the shape of boats; one cottage, indeed, is topped with a genuine boat. There were a few chimneys, but smoke came pouring from the doors, from holes in the thatch and walls. Many of the roofs bore a luxuriant growth of grass, with here and there a clump of daisies or of the yellow flowers which give color to Highland roads. But this was all the green we saw on their hill-side of rock and mud.

Through open door-ways we had glimpses of dark, gloomy interiors, dense with smoke. We did not cross a threshold, however; to seek admittance seemed not unlike making a show of the people's misery. The women and girls who passed in and out, and stood to stare at us, looked strong and healthy. Theirs is a life which must either kill or harden. Many were handsome, with strangely foreign, gypsy-like faces, and so were the bonneted men at work on the pier. It may be that there is truth in the story which gives a touch of Spanish blood to the people of the Outer Hebrides. If the ships of the Armada went down with all their treasure, it is said that their crews survived, and lived and took unto themselves wives in the islands, from which chance of deliverance was small. We heard only Gaelic spoken while we were at Castle Bay. The people of Great Britain need not go abroad in search of foreign parts; but an Englishman who only wants to see the misery and wrongs of nations foreign in name as well as in reality, would find little pleasure in Barra.

When we left the steamer the four sportsmen were getting off with their baggage, of which there was no small quantity. When we returned, hours later, they were getting in again. The one hotel in Barra was full. For consolation, I suppose, they shut themselves up in their state-room, and changed their trousers for the third time that day.

Their return brought to an end our bargaining for their state-room. The night in the ladies' cabin was one long nightmare. The steamer pitched and tossed as if she were still crossing the open Atlantic. At the many stopping-places there was a great noise of loading and unloading. At

TOWN OF BARRA.

midnight a mother, with her two babies and nurse, came to fill the unoccupied berths.

J——, in the saloon, fared little better. But the advantage of the restless night was that it sent us up on deck in time to see the eastern hills grow purple against the golden light of coming day. As in the evening, there was still land on either side. All the morning we went in and out of lochs and bays, and through sounds, and between islands. Indeed, I know of no better description of the Outer Hebrides than the quotation given in the guide-book: "The sea here is all islands and the land all lakes." And the farther north we went, the drearier seemed this land—a fitting scene for the tragedy enacted on it, which, though now many years old, is ever young in the memory of the people; for it was here in Uist that, in 1851, men and women were hunted like beasts, tracked by dogs to the caves and wilds where they lay in hiding, bound hand and foot, and cast upon ships waiting to carry them against their will across the Atlantic. We might have thought that no life had been left upon the islands but for an occasional wire fence, a sprinkling of sheep on the greener hill-sides, and lonely cottages, with thin clouds of blue peat-smoke hovering over them to show that they were not mere rocks. Once, stretching across the wilderness we saw telegraph poles following the coast-line. It is wise to let them make the best showing possible. Some of the islands are cut off telegraphically from the rest of the world.

We stopped often. At many of the landings not a house was to be seen. As a rule, there was no pier. The steamer would give her shrill whistle, and as it was re-echoed from the dreary hills huge black boats came sailing out to meet us. Instead of boats waiting for the steamer, as in the Mississippi, here she waited for them. And when they had dropped their sails, and rounded her bows and brought up alongside her lower deck, there tumbled into them men and women, and loaves, and old newspapers, and ham bones, and bits of meat, for in the islands there are always people on the verge of starvation.

At Loch Maddy, in North Uist, the brave warriors left us, and other sportsmen in ulsters and knickerbockers, and with many fishing-rods, came to take their place. On shore stood a man in plain, unassuming kilt, in which he looked at home. We liked to fancy him a laird of Uist in ancestral dress, and not like the youth at Oban, a mere masquerader. We asked the purser who he was.

"Oh, that is Mr. O'Brien, of Liverpool," was his answer.

Everybody had come up on deck, for the day was comparatively fine. It kept clearing and clouding, the sun now shining on the far hills

MOUNTAINS OF HARRIS, FROM TARBET.

and the rain pouring upon us; but again the showers were swept landward, and we were in sunshine. As we neared

HARRIS,

a little old lady came bustling up. When the steamer stopped in the Sound the men in the boats all touched their bonnets to her, a few even got on board to speak to her. She was better than a guide-book, and told the passengers near her all about Harris. She explained the difficulties of the channel through the Sound, which, like all Hebridean waters, is full of islands and rocks hidden at high tide, and is unprotected by lights. She pointed out Rodil Church, whose gray tower just showed above the green hills. She always called this bit of Harris the Switzerland of the Hebrides, she said. And with its checker-board-like patches of green and yellowing grain between the hills and the water, and lying, while we were there, in sunshine, it might have looked bright and even happy, but for the wretched cottages, of which there were more in this one place than we had seen on all the journey from Iona.

Once, as we watched the boats rounding the steamer's bows, we found ourselves next to this old lady. She seemed so glad to talk that we asked her could she perhaps tell us if the people of Harris were as miserable as their cottages.

"Oh," she said, "their condition is hopeless!" And then she went on to tell us that she lived only for Harris, and that there was no one who knew better than she its poverty. She was, we learned afterwards, Mrs.—or Mistress, as Lowlanders on board called her—Thomas. Her husband had been a Government surveyor in the island, and since his death she had interested herself in the people, among whom, for many years, she made her home.

The story of Harris, as she told it and as we have since read it in the report of the Commission of 1883, is in the main that of all the Islands and Highlands. It is the story of men toiling on land and sea, that by the sweat of their brow they may make, not their own bread, but the venison and game of others. Thousands starve that two or three may have their sport. The land in the Hebrides is barren, it is argued in behalf of the sportsmen. Harris is the barrenest of all, Mrs. Thomas declared. We could see this for ourselves; after the Switzerland of the Hebrides, the mountains rose a solid mass of black rock with scarce a trace of vegetation. But even Harris once supported its people. That was before they were made to share the land with the deer. To-day a few valleys and hill-sides are overcrowded, crofts divided and subdivided; while others once as green are now purple with heather, and silent save for the guns of sportsmen. Deer forests and large farms grow larger and larger; crofts shrink, until from the little patch of ground, long since overworked, the crofter can no longer reap even that which he sows. And yet he sees better land, where perhaps once grew his potatoes and grain, swallowed up in the cruel moors. While his harvest is starvation, deer and grouse live and multiply.

Many villages were cleared when the great deer forest of Harris was extended, not so many years ago. The people were turned from homes where they had always lived, the old with the young, and women about to become mothers. Highlanders love their land. Many went back again and again, even after their cottages were but black piles of ruin. Because he evicts tenants who will not pay their rent, the Irish landlord is called cruel. The evicted in the Hebrides have hitherto been those who interfere with the landlord's convenience or amusement. The rent has had nothing to do with it. And yet of Scotch evictions but comparatively little has been heard. Journalists skilled in their trade have published abroad, from one end of the land to the other, the tale of Irish wrongs. But who knows the injustice that has been done in Scotland in order to lay waste broad tracts of good ground? "I will tell you how Rodil was cleared," said John McDiarmid, of Scalpa, to the Commissioners. "There were one hundred and fifty hearths in Rodil. Forty of these paid rent. When young Macleod (the landlord) came home with his newly married wife to Rodil, he went away to show his wife the place, and twenty of the women of Rodil came and met them, and danced a reel before them, so glad were they to see them. By the time the year was out—twelve months from that day—these twenty women were weeping and wailing, their houses being unroofed and their fires quenched by the orders of the estate. I could not say who was to blame, but before the year was out one hundred and fifty fires were quenched."

As in Rodil, so it was where now stretches the deer forest of Harris—wherever, indeed, deer are hunted in the Highlands. Whoever wants to learn the nature of some of the blessings which come to the many from the proprietary power and right of the few—a right and power to which the Duke of Argyll refers all advance in the Highlands—let him read the "History of the Highland Clearances" as told by Alexander Mackenzie, the "Gloomy Memories of the Highlands," by Donald Macleod, himself one of the evicted. Their story is too cruel for me to tell again. Their country was desolate; their cities were burned with fire; their land, strangers devoured it in their presence, and it was desolate. Never did negro slaves in the South fare as did the Highland men and women cleared from the glens and valleys of Sutherland. Slaves at least represented so much money; but the crofter was and *is* less valuable to the laird than his sheep and his deer. Slaves could be sold. This was the one thing which the landlord, despite all his rights, could not do with his crofters. He could burn their cottages, starve them and their families, turn them adrift, and chase them over seas, there perhaps to meet anew starvation, disease, and death. From every part of the Highlands and Islands, from Ross and Argyllshire, as from Sutherland, hundreds and thousands were forced to fly, whether they would or not.

And with those who stayed at home, how fared it? The evicted squatted, we would call it, on the crofts of friends and relations in other parts of the estate. There was no place else for them to go. When there, they sought to solve the bitterest problem of life—how to make that which is but enough for one serve for two—and therein were unsuccessful. The landlord washed his hands of them and their poverty. They had brought it upon themselves, he reasoned; if crofts were overcrowded, the fault was theirs. You might as well force a man into the jungle or swamp reeking with malaria, and then when he is stricken upbraid him for living in such a hot-bed of fever. Mr. Alfred Russel Wallace does not exaggerate when he says, "For a parallel to this monstrous power of the land-owner, under which life and property are entirely at his mercy, we must go back to mediæval, or to the days when, serfdom not having been abolished, the Russian noble was armed with despotic authority, while the more pitiful results of this landlord tyranny, the wide devastation of cultivated lands, the heartless burning of houses, the reckless creation of pauperism and misery out of well-being and contentment, could only be expected under the rule of Turkish sultans or greedy and cruel pashas."

Emigration is the principal remedy suggested. The landlords of old enforced it, and now, for very shame, are content to commend it. It is the remedy most to their taste. It would leave them alone with their sheep and their game. If the only Highlanders were the gillies and shepherds, there would be an end of bothersome tales of wrongs, rousing the sympathy of the public. The real reason for emigration is that "any remedies which might be expected from land law reform or land acts will be and are likely to be long deferred, while in the mean time the people are dying like dogs from starvation." It has been urged that it would be better if many of the Islanders, like men of the east coast, became fishermen altogether and gave up their land. But if they did, the gain would not be theirs. In many lochs and bays the people are not allowed to fish for food because gentlemen must fish for pleasure.

Few have boats for deep-sea fishing; none have money to buy them. As it is, in the Long Island they must compete with well-equipped fishing-smacks sent into northern seas from Billingsgate markets.* Not only this, but in both Harris and Lewis, piers and harbors are few, and fishing-boats must be light that fishermen may pull them up on shore beyond reach of the tide. In parts of the northern Highlands people have been removed from the glens to the shores in hopes that they would become fishermen; but they were given no boats, no harbors.

For Skye and the Long Island, the nearest way to the main-land is by Strome Ferry, where the entrance to the harbor is intricate, and so poorly lighted that once the short winter days set in, as its passage cannot be attempted after dark, traffic between the islands and the main-land is seriously interrupted. But indeed one can but wonder at the few light-houses on this dangerous west coast. Here and there one erected on a lonely rock far out at sea is a triumph of engineering skill. But the most difficult channels, the wildest coasts, are left without a light. In the course of our long journey in Hebridean waters I think we saw but half a dozen. The life-boat institution

---

* I have just heard that Americans are about to send fishing-vessels over to these waters.

in British islands is now supported by charity. It seems as if the light-house service as well must fall to the benevolence of advertisers and city corporations.

It is well to say what the people ought to do; it is better to explain what they cannot do. They are hampered and held back on every side, and then the stranger is told that he need not pity them, they are so lazy. They are thriftless and good-for-nothing, Lowlanders on the steamer assured us. When you first go among them you believe in their laziness. Their little patches of potatoes and grain are full of weeds, and their ditches are choked; broken windows are mended with rags or heather, dirt and rubbish lie waiting to be cleared away. From their doors they step into the mud. A very little industry is needed to set these things right. You wonder if, after all, it may not be their own fault that they are so poor. But this is what a doctor of Raasay told the Commissioners, "The prevailing disease is poverty, and the chief remedy is food." The people have not enough to eat; that is why they do not work hard. You have but to look into their faces to know that they are starving. Hardly a winter passes that food has not to be begged for them. Even as I write, petitions come from a school-master in Lewis. Unless money and meal are sent to them, the people in his district cannot live through the winter.

But until two years ago had they not been from morning to night, from night to morning, weak from hunger; if fields had been made to yield a richer harvest; if crofts and houses had been kept neat and pretty, the profit would have been the landlords'. The greater the people's industry, the higher the rent they paid. If they made improvements, the rent was raised. Nor did they know at what moment the fruits of their labor might be swept away. The landlord had but to say, "I want my land, you must go," and their work of years had come to naught. No matter how long the crofter lived in the cottage where dwelt his father and grandfather before him, the day never came when he could say of a surety, "To-morrow this roof will be over my head, these fields and pastures will be mine to care for."

In the Hebrides, the landlord has always had rights; the crofter, until the passing of the Crofters' Bill of 1886, had none. I remember that on that day on the boat, with the shores of hopeless Harris in sight, Mrs. Thomas said to me, "There are two sides to the question, of course. The landlord has a right to do as he chooses with his own land." This is the argument of the landlords. They can quote Scripture in its support. "A man may do as he likes with his own," an Irish land-owner reminded his tenants the other day when he threatened to sweep them off the face of his estates. It is an old, well-worn argument; to answer it French revolutions and American civil wars have been fought. Englishmen have been ever ready to dispute it abroad; at home they are its advocates.

Probably we ought to have seen this other side; I admit that it would have been far pleasanter. A few letters of introduction—at that time, at any rate, not impossible to obtain—would have opened the doors of many of the big houses on our route, would have furnished J—— with a gun and me with days of boredom, would have introduced us to the natives in another fashion; for, according to all accounts, they would then have greeted us as if they were slaves, and not the most fearless and independent people in Great Britain. Of course we understand that strangers in the islands who do see this side of island life, find it as delightful as strangers in the South at home once found that of the old Southern gentleman. But we defy any one who visits the islands after our manner, not to be filled as we were with the thought of the people's misery; for the bondage in which they are held to-day is more cruel than was that of slaves in the slave States of America or of serfs in Russia.

There are good landlords in the Highlands, just as there were bad slave-owners in the South—men who give the half-starved, half-frozen crofter the

GATHERING PEAT.

blankets and meal which, if he were emancipated, he could provide for himself; for the crofter is no better, but indeed worse than a slave, since he must bear the burdens both of freedom and of slavery. He is free to pay more for land than it is worth, to be taxed for roads which are never built, and for schools where his language is scorned, and, in some islands, his religion dishonored; and, moreover, in proportion to his means, to be taxed more heavily than men in any other part of Scotland; in some districts he is free to cut from the moorland peat for fuel, to gather from the shore sea-weed for manure, to take from waste lands heather or grass to thatch his roof, only if he pays for the privilege. Here his freedom ends. In his house—the Englishman's castle—he is so little his own master that he cannot keep a sheep or a pig or a dog, unless it be the will of his laird. If he asks to lay his grievances before the factor he is called a rebel, and warned not to dare speak in such fashion; and this by a landlord praised by the great world because of the winter distribution of blankets and meal. If his complaints should be listened to, there is little chance of redress from men who value rabbits and grouse more highly than they do their tenants. He is wholly at the mercy of the factor, who usually holds all the highest offices on the estate, and has the power, as at Barra, to disenfranchise an entire island. This is the account of his position given by a minister in Skye: "The crofter has no protection from the large tacksmen; if he makes a complaint he can get no redress. There is no law in Skye. Might is the only right, and that, too, in the last decade of the nineteenth century. One great evil which sadly needs reform is the state of terrorism under which the small tenantry live through the insolent threats of subordinate officials, whose impudence increases in proportion to the smallness of their authority." It was time, indeed, when the Royal Commission was sent to the Highlands; and yet, though the Commission has reduced rents and cancelled arrears, it has not struck at the root of the evil—the existing relations between landlord and crofter.

The crofter's representative in Parliament is often, fortunately not always, a stranger who comes just before or after his election—as a candidate for Skye came to that island while we were there—and tells the people he has never been there before, they do not know him as yet, but he hopes they may later; and then he steams away in his yacht. Whether elected or not, we may feel sure he will never come again. But what is to be hoped for from Parliament? "They are all landlords in the House of Commons: what will they do for us?" the crofters and cotters of Lewis asked the other day. That is why they are taking matters into their own hands. They know there is no one else to help them. In a body they marched upon deer forest and sheep farm, and scattered over the island or drove into the sea sheep and deer. When there were no more sheep and deer, the landlord would be glad enough to give them back land which in days of old was green with their crops. And now, in further proof of the justice done to crofters, the leaders of these raids await trial in Edinburgh, to which town they cannot afford to bring their witnesses, and where no lawyers of note will defend them.*

The crofter is a slave not only to landlord and factor, but often to the merchant. The Englishman, when he finds the truck system far from home, cannot too strongly revile it. A report has but come from Newfoundland declaring that because of it a Newfoundlander is no more master of his own destiny than was a mediæval serf or a Southern negro in 1860. The writer need not have gone 1600 miles to the colonies to expose an evil which exists in the British Isles but 600 miles from London.† The Duke of Argyll regrets that it is employed in Tiree. His power as proprietor, the one power for good on his estates, stops short most unaccountably where other people

---

* I have explained elsewhere the result of this trial.
† A Truck Act has been passed which has somewhat modified the system in the Hebrides, but, as we have learned from a reliable source, it has not proved effectual.

might think it could be exercised to best advantage. Many Western Islanders, like Newfoundlanders, are bound hand and foot to the merchant. The latter provides them on credit with all the necessaries of life, often the poorest in quality, but always the highest in price. In return the crofter's earnings, before he has gained them, belong to the merchant, who, moreover, is at times his employer as well as his creditor. In Harris the women support their families by weaving the famous Harris cloth. To Edinburgh and London tailors it brings good profit; to them, starvation wages, paid in tea or sugar or meal. No money is in circulation on the island. Harris people have given their consent to emigrate, and then at the last moment have been kept prisoners at home because of a debt of years against them.

As we lay by the island of Scalpa, not far from Tarbert, a man came on board from one of the boats. He had a roll of cloth under his arm. He gave it to Mrs. Thomas, and asked if some one on board would buy it. As we looked at it he said nothing, but the pitiful pleading of his eyes, and their more pitiful disappointment as he turned away with his cloth, told the story. She tried to dispose of *their cloth for them, Mrs. Thomas said; and we have since heard that she buys more from them than even the local merchant.

THE "DUNARA CASTLE."

The *Dunara Castle* finally anchored at

TARBERT.

The principal building in the village was the large white manse, half hidden in trees. A parson's first care, even if he went to the Cannibal Islands, would be, I fancy, to make himself, or have made for him at somebody else's expense, a comfortable home. There were also on the outskirts of the village two or three new, well-built cottages for men in Lady Scott's, the landlord's, direct service, and a large, excellent hotel, the only place in Tarbert where spirits could be bought. The rich may have their vices, though the poor cannot. Beyond was misery. Wherever we went in the island we found a rocky wilderness, the mountains black as I have never seen them anywhere else, their tops so bare of even soil that in the sunlight they glistened as if ice-bound. Here and there, around the lochs and sloping with the lower rocky hills, were weed-choked patches of grain and huts wreathed in smoke, their backs turned hopelessly to the road. Near Tarbert there was one burrowed out like a rabbit-hole, its thatched roof set upon the grass and weeds of the hill-side. Just below, in the loch, Lady Scott's steam-yacht came and went. Beyond, her deer forest, a range of black mountains, stretched for miles. Within sight and low on the water were the thick woods, in the heart of which stands her shooting-lodge. The contrast gave the last bitter touch to the condition of the people. They starve on tiny crofts, their only homes; their landlord holds broad acres as playground for a few short weeks.

The hovels were as cheerless within as without. I do not know why it is that one takes liberties with the poor which one would not dare take with the rich. It is no small evil of poverty that it is everybody's privilege to stare at it. The people of Harris are hospitable, and receive the stranger with courtesy, but you can see that they resent the intrusion. It is not, I fear, to our credit that curiosity got the better of our scruples. We knocked at a cottage door, one Sunday afternoon, J——, as an excuse, asking for a light. As we drew near we heard the voice of some one reading aloud. Now it was silenced, and a tall old man in his shirt-sleeves came to the door with an open Bible in his hands. Within, on the left, was the dwelling-room of the household; on the right, the stable, cattle, and family share the only entrance. Into the room, through a single pane of glass, one ray of daylight fell across the Rembrandt-like shadows. On the mud floor, at the far end, a fire of peat burned with a dull red glow, and its thick, choking smoke curled in clouds about the rafters and softened the shadows. We could just make out the figures of two women crouching by the fire, the curtained bed in the cor-

INTERIOR OF A WEAVER'S COTTAGE.

ner, the spinning-wheel opposite. All other details were lost in gloom and smoke. Until you see it for yourself, you could not believe that in our nineteenth century men still live like this. Miss Gordon Cumming says that to the spinning and weaving of the women "is due much of such comfort as we may see by a peep into some of their little homes." But our peep showed us only that women weave and men work in vain, and that to speak of comfort is mockery in a cottage of Harris, or, indeed, in any cottage we saw in any part of the islands, for all those we went into were alike in their poverty and their darkness. As a rule, the fire burned in the centre on a circle of stones, and over it, from the roof, hung chain and hook for the kettle. They have not changed one jot or tittle since, a century ago, they moved Pennant to pity.

As we left the hut on the hill-side, the first we visited, "I beg pardon," said the old crofter, who had not understood J——'s thanks. His words seemed a reproach. We felt that we should be begging his pardon. To force our way in upon him in his degradation was to add one more to the many insults he has had to bear. He stood at the door a minute, and then went back into the gloom of the low room, with its mud floor and smoky rafters, which he calls his home.

All day long, even when the sun shone, as it did

at intervals during our stay, Harris was a land of sorrow and desolation, but in the evening it became a land of beauty. The black rock of the mountain-side softened into purple shadows against the gold of sky and sea, and in this glory the hovels and the people and the misery disappeared. And when the sun sank behind the western waters and the gold faded, there fell a great peace over the island, and with it began the twilight, that lingered until it grew into the coming day.

It was on Sunday mornings that there was greatest stir in Tarbert. Then the people came from far and near to meet in the little kirk overlooking the loch. We were told that comparatively few were at home. This was the season when they go to the east coast, the men to the fishing, the women to the curing-houses; but we thought they came in goodly numbers as we watched them winding with the road down the opposite hill-side, and scrambling over the rocks behind the town. Boats one by one sailed into the loch and to the pier, bringing with them old women in clean white caps and tartan shawls, younger women in feathered hats and overskirts, men in bonnets and blue sailor-cloth. They were a fine-looking set of people, here and there among them a face beautiful with the rich, dark beauty of the South—all that is left of the Armada. As they came up upon the pier they stopped in groups under the shelter of a boathouse, for the wind was high, the men to comb their beards and hair, the women to tie one another's bonnet-strings and scarfs, to smooth one another's shawls. And all the time scarce a word was spoken; they were as solemn at their toilet as if already they stood in church.

The Islanders are as melancholy as the wilderness in which they live. The stranger among them never gets used to their perpetual silence. Their troubles have made them turn from the amusements they once loved. The pipes now seldom are heard in the Hebrides. Their one consolation, their one resource, is religion, and to them religion is a tragedy. Nowhere was the great conflict in the Church of Scotland fought with such intensity, such passion, as in Skye. That same Sunday in Harris, we met the people coming home over the hills, and still they walked each alone, and all in unbroken silence. And this Sabbath stillness lasts throughout the week.

It is not only in Mr. Black's novels you meet kings in the Lews. From out of the boats laden with worshippers there stepped the King of Scalpa. He is a Campbell, we were told; and what is more, if he had his rights it is he who would bear the Argyll titles, enjoy the Argyll wealth, instead of the Campbell who calls himself Duke and writes books in the castle at Inverary. His story is the usual romance of the Highlands: a murder, a flight, the succession of the younger brother to titles and estates, the descendants of the murderer, exiles in a far island. And so it is that the real Duke of Argyll is but a merchant in Scalpa. However, if the so-called Duke had nothing more serious to fear than the pretensions of the King of Scalpa, he might rest at ease. It is his right not to a name, but to the privilege to do with his own as he likes, that he must needs defend. He can afford to ignore the Campbells of the Outer Hebrides; but let him fight with his deadliest weapons against the crofters who to-day pay him rent. All the arguments he has set forth in "Scotland as it Was, and Scotland as it Is," in themselves are not enough to avert the day of reckoning which even to him, apparently, seems so near at hand.

We left Harris, as we came to it, in the *Dunara Castle*, and dropped anchor in the Bay of Uig, in

SKYE,

one morning while the day was still young. The shores were circled about with patches of grain and potatoes and many cottages; and Skye, as we first saw it, seemed fair and fertile after the rocks of Harris. Its people are little better off, however. It was here, about Uig, on the estates of Captain Fraser, that crofters rebelled in 1884 as those of Lewis are rebelling to-day. Their rents in many cases have been reduced, their arrears cancelled. But landlords as they exist, or crofters, must go before there can be more than negative improvement in the islands.

When we were rowed to the shore the landlord of the Uig Inn stood posing as modern warden of

DOING SKYE.

the brand-new round tower on the hill-top. He took our knapsacks, and set us on the way to the Quiraing.

A steep climb up a wooded corrie brought us to the moors, the long purple distances unbroken save for the black lines marking where the peat had been cut, and the black mounds where the cuttings had been piled at intervals along the road. Once we passed men and women loading a cart with them. Once we saw a rude shepherd's hut, on a little hillock, surrounded by sheep. And in the long walk, that was all! When we started across the moorland the sun shone and the morning was hot. When suddenly the moorland came to an end and gave way to the tall jagged rocks of the Quiraing, the sky was all gray and the mist fell fast behind us. We left the road for a foot-path, and at once lost our way. We scrambled over rocks, slipped up and down soft spongy hills, jumped streams, and skirted lochs, J—— stopping in the most impossible places to make notes. We were now ankle-deep in mud, now knee-high in wet grass and heather. The guide-book says the Quiraing cannot be described; I am sure I cannot describe it, for the simple reason that I did not see it. At first I was too much taken up in trying not to kill myself; when the climbing was a little less dangerous and I looked about me, there was nothing to be seen. The mist had hidden the top of the rocks and was rolling down fast towards us. J—— was very anxiously looking at the guide-book and at the sea. Suddenly he seized me and pulled me, panting, behind him, over bowlders, through bracken, down a hill as steep as a house, in our hurry starting avalanches of stones. Then he jumped into the bed of a stream, down which we rushed, up to our knees in water, to the loch at the bottom. It was a mad flight. But by this time we could not see our hands before us.

"I am half dead," said I.

"If you don't come on we'll both be dead," said J——.

And just then, more by good luck than good management, we found ourselves on a road.

J—— had studied the lay of the land before our start. He knew this must be the road by the coast, twice as long on its way to Uig as that over which we had come; but there was no finding our way back in the mist. It fell from above, it rose from the ground, it closed about us on all sides. In a few minutes cloaks and hoods were soaked. We tried to be as indifferent as the Highlomaniac who pretends he likes this sort of thing. We sat on a stone by the way-side to eat the few sandwiches we had brought with us, and declared it an excellent joke. We walked across a dripping field as calmly as if it had been dry land, so that we might not come face to face with a monstrous bull which kept our path. And when the road came out close to the sea, and the mist turned into a driving rain, J—— even pulled out his guide-book and on its back made mysterious scrawls, which he said represented Duntulm Castle, a gray ruin on a high cliff, looking seaward.

There were by the road many groups of huts black, soaked, chimneyless; always near them a large manse and sometimes a larger school-house, which the people must maintain if they starve for it. Women with hunger on their faces looked after us. Children with old brown bags tied about their waists for all clothing stood at the doors to watch, but not one smiled at the sight. And yet we must have been funny! And the villages were silent as the moorland. There was not a voice to be heard. The women to whom we spoke shook their heads; "No English," was their only answer. The one person we found who could talk it was a man, and he had so many gutturals we could scarce understand him.

Near Duntulm Castle was a shooting-lodge; on the water a steam-yacht lay at anchor. The slave-driver is found for at least six weeks in the midst of his slaves.

We arrived at the inn about three in the afternoon, drenched and weary. A room was ready for us, a bright fire burning on the hearth. They always expected people to come home wet, the landlord's daughter said. She carried off our wet clothes; she lent me a dress; she brought us hot whiskey and water. One must be thoroughly tired to know what comfort means.

We had our tea with two English maiden ladies of the species one meets in Swiss and Italian pensions. We sat in a well-warmed room at a well-spread table. In the black, smoky huts half-starved men, women, and children were eating dry oatmeal; a few, perhaps, drinking tea with it. This is the extravagance with which the crofters have been reproached. They buy, or rather go into debt for, tea and sugar as well as meal, and therefore their landlords think them prosperous. They have never been so well off before, the Commissioners were told; once they lived on shell-fish throughout the summer. Yes, it was true, a minister of Snizort admitted, they did drink tea. But the people have no milk, now pasture-land has been taken from them. The landlord needed it for his large sheep farms and deer forests. I suppose they should go back to the shell-fish as of old. If they have food to eat, why complain of its quality? If this be so, if crofters of to-day, compared to their ancestors, live in luxury, then has the time indeed come when something should be done for them. Who will call them lazy or indifferent who has considered what the life of the Islander has been for generations? The wonder is that he has energy enough to keep on living.

We went the next day to

DUNVEGAN.

The road lay over long miles of moors, with now and then beautiful distant views of the mountains of Harris, but pale blue shadows on the western horizon, and of the high peaks of the Cuchullins, dark and sombre above the moorland.

Here and there at long intervals we came to the wretched groups of cottages we had begun to know so well. Old witch-like women and young girls passed, bent double under loads of peat or seaweed, so heavy that were the same thing seen in Italy, English people would long since have filled columns of the *Times* with their sympathy. As it is, these burdens are accepted as a matter of course, or sometimes even as but one of the many picturesque elements of Highland life. From one writer one hears of the Skye lassies, half hidden under bundles of heather, stopping to laugh and chatter; from another of Lewis women knitting contentedly as they walked along with creels, bearing burdens that would have appalled a railway porter of the south, strapped to their backs. We saw no smiles, no signs of contentment. On the faces of the strongest women there was a look of weariness and of pain. But perhaps the most pathetic faces in this land of sorrow were those of the children, already pinched and care-worn. I know others who have felt this even as we did. An Englishman who last summer spent a week in Skye has since told us how day after day he and his wife went upon their excursions lunchless, because in the first village to which they came they emptied

A REAL HIGHLAND LASSIE.

their luncheon-basket among the half-naked, half-starved children they found there. They could not bear the sight of the hungry little faces. But even in his sympathy, the general poverty seemed to him only right, he said, since it is in such perfect harmony with the dismal, dreary land in which the people live. If they were happy, however, if moors and hills were green with their crops, would it still seem so dismal?

That day and those which had preceded and those which followed we went into many huts, talked to many people. We became bold because we wished to learn for ourselves the truth of what we had heard, and not to be prejudiced by hearsay. The crofter's hut is felt to be a disgrace to the Highlands. The landlord shifts all responsibility. The crofter alone is at fault; he has no shame in living in his hovel, which is scarcely fit to shelter a dog. This is the favorite argument. How the crofter, without money, without other materials than those at his disposal, could build anything better has not as yet been explained. If, however, he does contrive to make it better, his rent is raised, and he might, until within two years, have been turned out on the morrow. If he moves into a house set up by a landlord there is again question of higher rent, though he may find it has been put up so cheaply that cold winds pour through cracks and crannies, heavy rains soak through roof and walls. In his own black hut, if he lives with his cattle he can at least keep warm. His contentment in his degradation is a myth. To many cottages we were absolutely refused admittance. Ours was not the experience of Miss Gordon Cumming. Whenever we approached a cottage, a kindly voice did not bid us welcome. I remember one in particular where the door was shut against us. Of a woman of the village who could speak English—

and it must be borne in mind that with few rare exceptions people in the Hebrides speak but Gaelic —and who had already shown us her smoky, dismal home, we asked that we might be let in to see the old loom. No, was the first answer sent out; its owner will not be dressed. No, was the second; the loom will not be working. No, was the third and final; "we wass just pretending about the loom; it wass the house we wanted to see." In another, though the woman drew up chairs by the peat smouldering and smoking in the middle of the floor, there was no mistaking she looked upon us as intruders. She shook her head and said without a smile, "No English," when we spoke to her; and then she turned her back and began to comb her hair. A bright, fresh-looking girl who rowed us over the water near Kingsburgh House received us more amiably. It was the usual interior, thick with smoke, all details lost in black shadow, though without the sun was shining. "You will find our houses very queer places to live in," she said. And as she ferried us across, every few minutes she turned and asked if we didn't find their cottages queer homes.

Nothing is left of Flora Macdonald's house which has made Kingsburgh famous. But our ferry-woman pointed to a clump of trees on the shores of the loch where it once stood. "Flora Macdonald was a good friend of the people," she said; "she was a strong woman and clever, and she helped to hide Prince Charlie from those who were in search of him, and for that reason she will be loved and remembered."

Strange as it may seem, these were her words. They so struck us at the time that I wrote them down once we were on shore again. I have heard people wonder at the intelligence Italian peasants show in expressing themselves; but it is not more striking than that of Western Islanders. When they could speak English, it always made us marvel. No one can read the report of their evidence before the Royal Commission without marvelling with us.

It was not only in Skye we talked to the people; already in Harris we had much to say to those who had the English. The very fact that we were walking, a great part of the time with packs on our backs, made the people meet us on more friendly terms than if we drove in coaches or sailed in yachts. We were strangers, it was evident; but we were not sportsmen or moneyed tourists. On every side we heard the same story of hated landlords and exhausted crofts. We know that what we say can have but little influence for good or evil. And yet when we remember the sad stories to which we listened, and the cruel lot of those who told them, we would not run the smallest risk of making that lot still more cruel, those stories still more sad. There is ill-feeling enough between Hebridean landlords and their slaves. In three cases at least crofters were turned from their crofts because they gave evidence to the Commissioners of 1883. It is well to be on the safe side. The chances are, not a landlord will know that we have been writing about his estates after walking over them; but we think it best to give no clew to the identity of men who told us in a friendly way that which already had been proclaimed officially.

The chief complaint was the same wherever we went: "We have not enough land; we could and would pay rent willingly if we had more ground to cultivate. As it is, our crofts are not large enough to keep us in food." The outside world has been busy watching the battle in Ireland; little attention has been spared to the Highlands; yet every small paragraph on the subject for which newspapers can make room, between accounts of stolen breeches and besieged members of Parliament, shows the determination of the men who are fighting the same battle in the far north. If troops are kept in Ireland, if Welsh tithes can only be collected by hussars, war-ships are sent to the Islands. If Irishmen, protected by a Land League, refuse to pay rent, so do Scotch crofters. Indeed, the latter are far more determined and daring. They know, too, how to hold together. In Glendale, an out-of-the-way corner of Skye to which strangers seldom

penetrate, not a crofter has paid rent for five years.
An old man, tenant on another estate, told us about
them with pride. "No, sir," he said, "they have
no paid a penny for five years, but the factor he
will keep friends with them. He will know ferry
well if he wass not their friend it will be worse
trouble that will be coming whatever."

He was a fine, healthy old man, between sixty
and seventy; and when he found that we sympa-
thized, he walked about half a mile just to talk
with us. He pretended he came to show us the
way, but as the road was straight before us it was
easy to see through his excuse.

J—— asked him what he thought about the crofter question. "I will be a real old Land Leaguer
every time," he declared; and then he went on to
tell us that in his part of the island the crofters
held together like one man. The Commission was
coming; it was slow, but they would wait for it.
Then, if it did not improve their condition, they
would take matters into their own hands. Their
landlord was good enough, as landlords went; he
was a civil-spoken gentleman if rents were paid on
the very day they were due, but that was about all
that could be said for him. Rents were not so
high on his estate as on others, but the taxes were
heavy, and it was more land they needed. "You
will see those potatoes"—and he pointed to a tiny
green patch sloping down from the road to a ditch,

beyond which was heather—" you will see for yourself they grow well whatever. And they would be growing as well on the other side of the ditch, where I myself have planted them in other days.

DUNVEGAN CASTLE.

But what will grow there now? Heather and ferns! And it will be heather and ferns you will see as far as you can for twelve miles. If they will be giving us more land, sir, it's no trouble from the Highlanders they will be having; but if they don't give it to us we will take it."

He shook hands heartily with us both when he left. One may doubt the demagogue who uses the people's suffering for political capital; but one can but respect a man like this sturdy old crofter, himself one of the people, who knows his wrongs and determines to right them. His methods may be illegal; so have been those of many men who have struggled for freedom.

At Dunvegan Inn we were again in civilized society. We dined with two young men from London who were followed even here by the *Saturday Review* and the *Standard*. They took interest in the evicted Irish, and ignored the existence of Highland crofters; they could tell us much of the fish, but nothing of the fishermen. They were anxious to direct us to many howling wildernesses within an easy walk of the dinner-table, where we could escape from the people; and when the people, in the shape of two Aberdeen farmers, full of the crofter's wrongs, appeared at breakfast, they went from the room in disgust. I think this disgust would have been greater had they known how much more interesting we found the farmers.

Beyond the inn the road led through a dense wood to the castle of the Macleod of Macleod. Trees will not grow on Hebridean soil until the laird wishes to raise them for himself; then they thrive well enough. Of course we did not expect to find them growing on northern exposed shores; but surely there must be other sheltered spots besides those directly around the laird's house. However, it is the same with his crops; broad acres are covered by his grain and that of his large tenants; his pasture-land is fresh and green. It is a strange fact that only when the crofter asks to cultivate the land does it become absolutely barren. It is but a step from the wild, lonely moorland to the beautiful green wood at Dunvegan. Landward it shuts in the castle, whose turreted keep rises high above the ivy-grown battlemented walls, crowning a rocky island in a sheltered corner of the loch. The water has been drained from the natural moat, but the rock falls sheer and steep from the castle gate, and the drawbridge still crosses the gulf below. We did not go inside; we were told that the present wife of the Macleod objected to visitors, even though she admitted them. We believe there are tapestries and old armor and the usual adjuncts to be seen for the asking, such things as one can find in any museum; but it is only by going to the islands that you can see the crofters' wrongs.

Almost at the end of the woods, and yet sheltered by them, was a pretty old-fashioned flower-garden, surrounded by well-clipped hedges, and as well cared for as the garden of an English castle. Nearer to the inn, on a low hill, was the graveyard of the Macleod. We pushed open the tumble-down gate and squeezed through. A hundred years ago Dr. Johnson found fault with the bad

English on Lord Lovat's tomb; to-day we could hardly find the tomb. The stone on which the inscription was carved lay in pieces on the ground. It may be that the Macleod of Macleod has bankrupted himself to save his tenants from starvation.

GRAVEYARD OF THE MACLEOD.

This is most praiseworthy on his part. But we could not help thinking that if he and all the Macleods, from one end of Great Britain to the other, are so anxious to be buried here, they might among them find money enough to free the enclosure of their dead from the whiskey bottles and sandwich tins left by the tourist. The resting-place of the dead Macleod lies desolate; not far off is the garden, with smooth lawn and many blossoms. A few flowers less, perhaps, and at least the bottles and tins that defile what should be a holy place, could be cleared away. And this graveyard, with its broken tombs and roofless chapel, is a ruin of yesterday. A century ago Dr. Johnson saw it still cared for and in order. The people in Dunvegan told us that twenty years since the roof fell in; it has never been repaired. We have been to the graveyard of old St. Pancras in London, where every few minutes trains rush above the desecrated graves; but here the dead are unknown, or else, like Mary Wolstonecraft and Godwin, their tombs have been removed beyond the reach of modern improvements. We have been to the Protestant burying-ground in the cemetery of old St. Louis in New Orleans, neglected because those who lie there belong to the despised faith. And yet neither of these is dishonored as is the graveyard where sleep the Macleods of the far and near past, whose greatness the living Macleods never cease to sing. Beneath the weeds are old gray slabs, with carvings like those of Iona; in the ruined weed-grown chapel walls are fresh white marble tablets. At Dunvegan the dead are not forgotten, not despised; they are only neglected. The mower comes and cuts the long grass from above their trampled graves. Let the laird make hay while the sun shines, for the day is coming when the storms, forever brooding over the Isle of Mists, will break forth with a violence he has never felt before, and he and his kind will be swept away from off the face of the land.

To-day Macleod of Macleod is a poor man. One year of famine, to keep the crofters from starving, he emptied his own purse. It is but another proof of the uselessness of charity in the Hebrides. What did it profit the crofters that Macleod became for their sake a bankrupt? They still starve. He who would really help them must be not only their benefactor, but their emancipator.

From Dunvegan to

STRUAN

it was all moorland. The shadeless road ran for miles between the heather, from which now and again, as we passed, rose the startled grouse. Far in front were the Cuchullins, only their high, jagged peaks showing above the clouds that hung heavy about them. The little Struan inn, which we had to ourselves, was low down by the water, at the foot of a wide hill-side planted with turnips. On the brow of the hill, like so many bowlders in the mud, were strewn the huts of a miserable village. Manse and kirk were at a becoming distance across the road.

Though this was after the 12th of August, when the Wilderness of Skye is supposed to be of some use, we saw in miles of moorland one man fishing, and a second shooting; for the latter a carriage waited on the road below. In order that these two, and perhaps half a dozen more like them, should have a fortnight's amusement, the land from Dunvegan to Sligachan has been cleared of its inhabitants. On the high-road between these two places—a distance of about twenty-two or twenty-three miles—there are not above a dozen huts, and only one or two decent houses. It is true, there is a large and flourishing distillery.

After Struan we were still on the moors. The only breaks in the monotony were the showers, the mile-stones, and the water-falls. The mountains, upon which we had counted for the beauty of the walk, were now completely lost in the clouds. Not until we were within two miles of Sligachan did the thick veil before them roll slowly up, showing us peaks rising beyond peaks, rugged hollows, and deep precipices. But it fell again almost at once, and for the rest of the way we saw but one high mountain coming out and being swallowed up again in the mist and clouds.

Near the inn, and a hundred yards or so from the road, was a reedy pool. A man stood in the water, a woman on the shore, both silently fishing in the rain. It is in duck-puddles like this—in which, were they at home, an American boy would sail his boat or throw his line to his heart's content

—that guests in Highland inns, by special kindness of the landlord, are allowed to fish, this permission being advertised as a leading attraction of the inn.

We intended to stay a day or two in

SLIGACHAN.

We wanted to see the Cuchullins and the much-talked-about Loch Coruisk. But here we found that we were again on the tourist route from which we had gone so far astray. There was not a room to be had in the inn. It was full of immaculately dressed young ladies and young Oxford men, all with their knickerbockers at the same degree of bagginess, their stockings turned down at the same angle. We might have thought that the landlady objected to tramps when the company was so elegant, had she not offered to put us up in the drawing-room and found places for us at the *table-d'hôte* luncheon. The talk was all of hotels and lochs and glens and travels. How long have you been in Skye? Is this your first visit? Did you come by Loch Maree? At what hotel did you stay in Oban? But there was not a word about cottages; for there is nothing in Sligachan, or near it, as far as we could see, but this swell hotel, which seemed very good.

Beds in the drawing-room meant to be at the mercy of the company. We did not hesitate.

And still the moors stretched out before us. No one who has not tramped in Skye can imagine its dreariness. In Portree, a miniature Oban, we lost all courage. We might have gone back to Loch Coruisk. We might have tramped to take a nearer view of the Old Man of Storr, which we had already seen in the distance. We might have walked to Armadale, or steamed to Strome Ferry. There were, in fact, many things we could and should have done; but we had seen enough of the miserable life in the islands—those great deserts, with but here and there a lovely oasis for the man of wealth. Our walks had been long; we were tired physically and sick mentally.

And so, early one morning, we took the boat at Portree and steamed back to the main-land; past Raasay, where Dr. Johnson stayed, and where there was a big house with beautiful green lawn and fine woods; past Glenelg, where we should have landed to follow the Doctor's route, but the prospect of a thirty miles' walk to reach the nearest inn made cowards of us; past Armadale, now as when Pennant saw it, "a seat, beautifully wooded, gracing most unexpectedly this almost treeless tract;" past one island of hills after another; and thus into the Sound of Mull, to get a glimpse of Tobermory in sunshine. It was a lovely day; sea and sky and far islands blue, the water like glass;

though, before it had come to an end, we had twice fled to the cabin from heavy showers. There were many sight-seers on board, and we could but wonder why. The women read novels, the men went to sleep. But they had done their duty — they had been to Scotland for the holidays; they had probably seen the Quiraing and Dunvegan. But they had not gone our way. The coach roads are those from which the least misery is visible.

That evening Oban did its best for us. The sun went down in red fire beyond Mull's now purpling hills. And as the burning after-glow cooled into the quiet twilight, we looked for the last time on the island of Mull. It seemed in its new beauty to have found peace and rest. May this seeming have become reality before we again set foot on Hebridean shores!

NOTE.—The Crofters' Act of 1886 was supposed to do away with the crofters' wrongs. As yet it has accomplished little. In some cases the Commissioners appointed for the purpose have lowered the extortionate rents which crofters have been starving for years to pay. Now that agitation in the islands has made it absolutely necessary that something should be done for the people, in one or two test cases, those clauses of the act which prevent landlords evicting tenants at their own pleasure have been enforced. Beyond this the condition of the people is absolutely no better than it was before the act was passed. They have not enough land to support them, and when they appeal for more, their landlord answers, as Lady Matheson has just answered her small tenants in the Lewis, "The land is mine; you have nothing to do with it." Nothing has been done for the cotters who have no land at all; nothing for fishermen, who are, if possible, worse off at the end of the fishing season than they were at the beginning. The money appropriated for the building of piers and harbors and the purchase of boats has not as yet been put to its proper use.

TO THE EAST COAST, AND BACK AGAIN.

ONE always hears of Highland scenery at its best; one usually sees it at its worst. We found the trip from Oban to Inverness up the Caledonian Canal as tedious as it is said to be charming. The day was gray and misty and rainy. In the first boat we sat in the cabin, in the second under an awning. Occasionally we went on deck to look for the sights of the journey.

As we steamed up Loch Linne a Scotchman pointed out Ben-Nevis.

"Well," said J——, critically, "if you were to put a top on it, it might make a fairly decent mountain."

After that we were left to find the sights for ourselves.

The day would have been unbearably dull but for the exertions of a Mr. Macdonell. He was, I am as ashamed to say as he seemed to be, our fellow-countryman. He did not look in the least like an American, nor like an Englishman, though his ulster, coat, trousers, collar, necktie, gloves, and hat were all so English. He was a middle-aged man, handsome, and gentlemanly enough until he began to talk. At the very start he told everybody on board in general and each individual in particular that he was a Macdonell. As all the people about here are Macdonells, no one was startled. The name in these parts is rather more common than, and about as distinguished as, Smith in the Directory.

"I'm a Macdonell," he said, "and I'm proud of it. It's a great clan. No matter what our nationality may be now, sir, we're all Macdonells still. I'll tell you the way we do in our clan. Not long ago one of the Macdonells of Lochaber was married. He was not very rich—he had about £12,000 a year perhaps—and the Macdonells thought it would be a nice thing to give him a present of money from Macdonells all over the world. There was not a Macdonell who did not respond. I was in Melbourne at the time, and I was proud to give my guinea. Now, how different it was with Grant, that man who was President of the United States. The clan Grant tried to do the same thing when one of their chief's family was married, and the factor sent to this Grant, and said they would be very proud and had no doubt he would be very glad to contribute to this happy occasion in the old clan. And what do you think he answered? He indorsed on the letter sent him—I saw it myself — that he was not one of the tenantry, and therefore would not contribute. That shows what a snob he was. But it's very different with the Macdonells. I'll tell you what happened to me the other day near Banavie. I lost one of my gloves; they were driving gloves—expensive gloves, you know. I gave the odd one to the driver, and said if he could find the other he would have a pair. The next day he came to me with both gloves. 'Sir,' he said, 'I cannot keep them; I too am a Macdonell!' I gave him the other glove and a guinea. That shows the fine clannish feeling."

We have heard that there is a proverb about fools and Americans.

Mr. Macdonell stood on the upper deck to look towards the country of the Macdonells, which he could not see through the mist. He took out his guide-book and read poetry and facts about his clan, to two American girls, until, quite audibly, they pronounced it all stuff and him a bore. He praised the Macdonell chiefs to Englishmen until they laughed almost in his face. "The Duke of New York," they called him before evening. He sang the praises of his Macdonell land to any one who would listen. "I like it better than Switzerland or our own country," he said; "I'm coming back next year to rent a shooting-place. But the trouble is the people here don't like us. It's the fault of men like Carnegie. He comes and gives them £20,000 for a library. And then what does he do? He makes a speech against their queen. It's shocking. It's atrocious."

I wonder why Americans, as soon as they borrow the Englishman's clothes, must add his worst traits to their own faults. "That kind of American," a Londoner on board said to us, "has all the arrogance and insolence of a lord combined with the ignorance and snobbishness of a cad." He was right. Of all the men who rent the great deer forests of Scotland, none are such tyrants as the American millionaires who come over, as Mr. Macdonell probably will next summer, for the shooting. More than one Scotchman we met told us so plainly. There is a famous case where the cruelty of an American sportsman, who plays the laird in the Highlands, so far outdid that of the real laird that the latter came forward to defend his people against it! Now that the war of emancipation is being fought from one end of Great Britain to the other, it is to our shame that there are Americans who uphold the oppressors. One might think we struggled for freedom at home only to strive against it abroad. Mrs. Stowe could write "Uncle Tom's Cabin" on behalf of slaves in the United States; in Great Britain she saw only the nobility and benevolence of the slave-driver. From the plantations of the South there never rose such a cry of sorrow and despair as that which rang through the glens and straths of Sutherland when men were driven to the sea to make room for sheep. And yet to Mrs. Stowe this inhuman chase was but a sublime instance of the benevolent employment of superior wealth and power in shortening the struggle of advancing civilization, and elevating in a few years a whole community to a point of education and material prosperity which, unassisted, they might never have attained. You might as well call the slavery of negroes a sublime instance of the power of traders to shorten the natural course of human development, since if left to themselves the blacks could not have advanced beyond the savage state in which they were found. I fear the American love for a lord is not exaggerated, if even Mrs. Stowe could be blinded by it.

There was little to break the monotony of the journey except the Macdonells. "If the sun only shone," Mrs. Macdonell explained, "there would be the lights and shadows." As it was, however, water and sky and shores were of uniform grayness. Now and then we passed the ruins of an old castle. At a place whose name I have forgotten the boat stopped that everybody might walk a mile or more to see a water-fall. It may have been our loss that we did not go with the rest; certainly a party of Frenchmen on their return declared it *une cascade vraiment charmante*. At Fort Augustus the boat was three-quarters of an hour getting through the locks, and in the mean time enterprising tourists climbed the tower of the new Benedictine monastery, which stands where was once the old fort. We went instead to the telegraph office, and secured a room in Inverness, and gave the landlord an order for the letters we hoped were waiting for us at the bank. Young Benedictines in black gowns, like students of the Propaganda on the Pincian, were walking out two by two.

These were the day's excitements.

As we neared Inverness, Mr. Macdonell was again on deck. "I always go to the Caledonian Hotel in Inverness," he told us. "What I like is to stay at the best hotels, where I meet the society of England and Scotland—the real society. There's the Royal Hotel in Edinburgh; it suits me because you are sure to find it full of good English and Scotch society. I must always have the best society. Besides, they're very good hotels, both of them. In our country we boast of the products of the Chesapeake; but we have nothing so delicious, nothing so delicate, as the fresh herring they will serve you for breakfast at the Caledonian."

As we drove from the boat to

INVERNESS,

we passed the stage of the Caledonian Hotel. In it sat the Macdonell with a family of Jews, and an

Englishman and his daughter who, throughout the journey, had shown themselves so superior, we should not wonder some day to find them behind the counter of an Oxford Street store. They were all on their way to mingle with the real society of England and Scotland.

It probably was a pleasure to Mr. Macdonell to find that the tobacconist next to the hotel, and the dry goods merchant but a few doors off, were his fellow-clansmen. In fact, every other banner—I mean sign—flung out on the outward walls of Inverness bore his name.

Our social pretensions were more modest. We went to the Station Hotel for comfort, and trusted to luck for society. In the great hall of the hotel we first realized the full extent of our shabbiness. Our knapsacks shrank out of sight of porters and maids. The proprietor was too busy distributing rooms to decently dressed travellers—the most gorgeous of whom gloried in his allegiance to the *Police Gazette* of New York—to notice us. But as he paused for a moment, J—— asked if there were any letters for Mr. Pennell. "Where is Mr. Pennell?" asked the proprietor, with interest. When he heard where he was, then came the transformation scene. Two gentlemen in dress-coats, each carrying a diminutive knapsack preceded us up the stairs; two gentlemen in dress-coats, each carrying a huge bundle of letters, the accumulation of weeks, followed us. We felt like a lord mayor's procession, but we did not look it. We were led into the best bedroom, but before the door was closed we thought we saw disappointment in the eyes of the proprietor. We at once consulted the tariff on the wall to learn what it cost to send a telegram in Scotland. We can only say that it did not prove very expensive, that the hotel was very good, that everybody was very attentive, and that the society may have been the best for all we knew.

The next morning we started on foot, all our baggage on our backs, to the disgust of the gentlemen in dress-coats. We walked at a good pace out of the town, and on the broad, smooth road that leads to Culloden. The country was quiet and pastoral, and the way, in places, pleasant and shady. It was a striking contrast to the western wilderness from which we had just come.

But twenty miles lay between us and Nairn; like Dr. Johnson, we were going out of our way to see Culloden Moor and Cawdor Castle. The road was too good. It set us thinking again of a tricycle on which we could travel at stimulating speed over country monotonous in its prosperous prettiness. Walking meant steady trudging all day, and a hasty glance at castle and moor when we came to them.

It was unbearable. Weeks of experience had

taught us all the drudgery of tramping, none of its supposed delights. We asked people we met if there was a cycle agent in Inverness. No one knew. Then the trees by the road-side gave place to open country with waving wheat-fields; and oh, how hot it grew! Peddlers whom we had passed—the only people, besides ourselves, we saw tramping in Scotland—overtook and passed us. Two men went by on bicycles. How cool and comfortable they looked! How hot and dirty and dusty and miserable we felt! This was too much.

"Confound this walking! If ever I walk again!" said J——; and, almost within sight of Culloden, he turned. After looking over to where I knew the moor must be, I meekly followed him, and in silence we went back to Inverness.

The roads about here being particularly good, there was not a cycle agent in the town. There was no getting a machine for love or money. It was now too late to attempt to walk to Nairn. There was nothing to do but to train it. In the interval of waiting we saw Inverness. It is a pretty city, with a wide river flowing through it, many bridges—one with a great stone archway—a new cathedral, and a battlemented, turreted castle high above the river. Clothes dry on the green bank that slopes down to the water's edge, women in white caps go and come through the streets, which, with their gabled houses, show that curious

French feeling found all over the East of Scotland, and even the costumes of the women help to carry it out.

In Inverness, and in fact all the way to Fraserburgh, J—— made many notes and sketches, the best, he says, of our journey. All but a few have been lost, and so the world will never enjoy them. This is sad, but true. If any one should happen to find the sketch-book he need not return it in hopes of a reward. J—— has no use for it at this moment. In fact, the finder had better keep it; it may be valuable some day.

When the train reached

NAIRN,

"Well," said J——, in triumph, "we've got through a day's work in half an hour;" and we dropped our knapsacks at the hotel and set out for Cawdor, which is five miles from the town.

The day so far had been fine. Once we were on the road again the sun went behind the clouds, mist fell over the country before us. A lady in a dog-cart warned us of rain, and offered us a lift. To make up for the morning's weakness, we refused heroically. There was nothing by the way but broad fields of grain, which seemed broader after the wretched little patches of Skye and Harris, and large farm-houses, larger by comparison with Hebridean hovels. When the roofs and gables of the castle came in sight, had we had our Macbeth at our fingers' ends, I have no doubt we might have made an appropriate quotation. A long fence separated two fields; on each post sat a solemn rook, and hundreds more made black the near grass. But we did not call them birds of ill-omen and speak of the past as we should have done; J—— only said it was right to find so many cawing things at the gate of Cawdor Castle.

I wish that we had found nothing worse. Just as we reached it the mist turned to heavy rain. This is the depressing side of sight-seeing in Scotland; you must take your holidays in water-proofs. J—— made several sketches, for the rain poured in such torrents our stay was long. We stood under the old gate-way and at the window of the porter's lodge. The sketches were very charming, very beautiful, but they are lost! We walked about in the rain and looked at the castle from every side. But as everybody who has travelled in Scotland has described Cawdor, there is no special reason why I should do it again. The sketches would have been original.

The most provoking part of it was that we had scarce left the castle a mile behind when the rain became mist again; at the third mile-stone we were once more in a dry world.

Boswell called Nairn "a miserable place." Dr. Johnson said next to nothing about it. Perhaps the people laughed at them as they did at us. We thought their manners miserable, though their town now is decent enough. It is long and narrow, stretching from the railway-station to the sea. After the hotels and shops, we came to the fishermen's quarter. The houses were mostly new; a few turned old gables and chimneys to the street. Women in white caps, with great baskets on their backs, strode homeward in the twilight. Everywhere brown nets were spread out to dry, boats lay along the sands, beyond was the sea, and the smell of the fish was over it all.

The next morning we learned from the maid that Macbeth's blasted heath was but a few miles from Nairn; all the theatricals went there, she said. We made a brave start; but bravery gave out with the first mile. Walking was even more unbearable than it had been the day before. There could be nothing more depressing than to walk on a public highway through a well-cultivated country under a hot sun. Already, when we came to the near village of Auldearn, we had outwalked interest in everything but our journey's end. We would not go an extra step for the monuments the guide-book directs the tourist to see, though the graveyard was within sight of the road.

Macbeth seems to have shared the fate of prophets in their own country. We asked a man passing with a goat the distance to Macbeth's Hill, as it is called on the map. He didna know, he answered. But presently he ran after us. Was the gentleman we spoke of a farmer? Another man, however, knew all about it. He had never been to the top of the hill; he had been told there were trees up there, and that it wasn't different from the other hills around. And yet he had heard people came great distances to see it. He supposed we had travelled far just to go up the hill. He knew from our talk, many words of which he couldna understand, that we were no from this part of the country. But then sometimes he couldna understand the broad Scotch of the people in Aberdeenshire. There were some people hereabouts who could talk only Gaelic. They had been turned off the Western Islands, and had settled here years ago, but they still talked only the Gaelic.

He went our way for half a mile or less, and he walked with us. His clothes were ragged, his feet bare, and over his shoulders was slung a small bundle done up in a red handkerchief. In the last three years, he said, he had had but two or three days' work. Work was hard to get. Here rents were high, farmers complained, and this year the crops were ruined because of the long drought. He did think at times of going to America. He had a sister who had gone to live in Pittsburg. It might be a good thing. There are Scotchmen who have done well in Pittsburg. He left us with minute directions. The hill, though not far from the road, which now went between pine woods and heather, could not be seen from it. We came to the point at which we should have turned to the blasted heath.

"It's a blasted nuisance," J—— said, and we kept straight on to the nearest railway-station.

This was Brodie. The porters told us there was a fine castle within a ten minutes' walk, and a train for Elgin in fifteen minutes. We waited for the train.

We were so tired, so disgusted, that everything put us out of patience. Even a small boy who had walked with us earlier in the morning to show us the way, simply by stopping when we stopped and starting when we started, had driven us almost frantic. I mention this to show how utterly wearisome a walking tour through beautiful country can be.

At the town of

ELGIN

we were in the humor to moralize on modern degeneracy among the ruins. A distillery is now the near neighbor of the cathedral. Below the broken walls, still rich with beautiful carving, new and old gravestones, as at Iona, stand side by side. In nave and transepts knights lie on old tombstones, under canopies carved with leaves and flowers; here and there in the graveyard without are moss-grown slabs with the death's-head and graceful lettering of the seventeenth century; near by are ugly blocks from the modern stone-mason. The guide-book quotes some of the old inscriptions; but it omits one of late date, which should, however, receive the greatest honor—that of the man who cared for the ruins with reverence and love until the Government took them in charge. These ruins are very beautiful. Indeed, nowhere does the religious vandalism of the past seem more monstrous than in Scotland. The Government official asked us to write our names in the Visitors' Book; he made it seem a compliment by saying that it was not everybody's name he wanted. We thought him a man of much greater intelligence than the Glasgow verger. He could see, he said, that J—— knew something about cathedrals and architecture.

We found nothing else of interest in Elgin. It had a prosperous look, and we saw not a trace of the old timbered houses with projecting upper stories of which Dr. Johnson writes. The remainder of our stay we spent in a restaurant near the station, where we talked politics with a farmer. He lectured us on free-trade. Scotch farmers cry for protection, he said, but they don't know what it means. Free-trade is good for the bulk of the people, and what would protection do for the farmer? Nothing! If he got higher prices, the landlord would say, Now you can afford to pay me higher rent, and he would pocket the few shillings' difference.

We talked with many other farmers in the east of Scotland. Sometimes we journeyed with them in railway-carriages; sometimes we breakfasted and dined with them in hotels. They all had much to say about protection and free-trade, and we found that Henry George had been among them. Their ideas of his doctrine of the nationalization of the land were at times curious and original. I remember a farmer from Aberdeenshire who told us that he believed in it thoroughly, and then explained that it would give each man permission, if he had money enough, to buy out his landlord.

After our lunch at Elgin we again got through a day's work in less than an hour. We went by train to

BUCKIE,

a place of which we had never heard before that afternoon. How J—— happened to 'buy tickets for it I cannot explain, since he never made it quite clear to me. We found it a large and apparently thriving fishing town, with one long line of houses low on the shore, another above on the hill, and a very good hotel, the name of which I am not sure we knew at the time; certainly we do not remember it now.

FISHER-BOATS HAULED UP NEAR BUCKIE.

It was at Buckie that J—— made several of the best sketches in the lost sketch-book in the evening as we watched the boats sail silently out from the harbor. The sun had just set. The red light of the after-glow shone upon the water. Against it, here and there, the brown sails stood out in strong relief. Other boats lay at anchor in the cool gray of the harbor.

In the morning we made a new start on foot. Now and then, for a short distance, the road went inland across treeless, cultivated country; but the greater part of the time it lay near the sea, and kept wandering in and out of little fishing villages, in each of which the lost sketch-book came into play. They were all much alike; there was usually the harbor, where the fishing-boats were moored, some with brown sails hung out to dry and flapping slowly in the breeze; others with long lines of floats stretched from mast to mast; and as it was not only low tide but near the end of the fishing season, all were drawn up in picturesque masses in the foreground, the light of sea and sky bright and glittering behind them. Carts full of nets, men and women with huge bundles of them on their backs, were always on their way either up or down the hill at whose foot the village nestled; or on the level at its top the nets were spread like great snares, not for birds, but for any one who tried to walk across them. Boxes and barrels of salted fish were piled along the street. In the air was the strong smell of herrings. In every village new houses were being or had just been built, but the soft gray smoke hovering above the roofs toned down their aggressive newness. In their midst was the plain white kirk.

There were so many villages that we could not complain of monotony; and then sometimes, on the stretch of beach beyond, dismantled boats in various stages of decline were pulled up out of reach of the tide. Sometimes on the near links men were playing golf. Once we passed three, each putting his little white ball on a bit of turf. They were very serious about it. "Now to business," we heard one say as we went by. But it grew very hot towards noon, and in the heat our first enthusiasm melted. When

NEAR CULLEN.

Cullen came in sight we were again declaring that nothing would induce us to walk another step.

However, a hearty lunch changed our minds. The truth is, we hated to give in. Though we were quite certain we would never tramp again, we were unwilling to confess our one walk a failure. At the hotel we were told that the road to Banff, our next stopping-place, kept inland, but the landlady thought that to the nearest village at least there was a path by the shore. A man on the outskirts of the town tried to dissuade us from going that way; there was such a brae to be climbed, he said. But there seemed no doubt about the path. When we persisted, he walked back with us to direct us the better, J—— talking to him about the brae as if he had never heard of a hill in his life, the man describing the difficulties before us as if ours was an Alpine expedition. The hill was steep enough. At the top there was no path, but instead a field of tall prickly furze, through which we waded. Oh, the misery of that five minutes' walk! At every step we were stung and pricked by hundreds of points sharper than needles. And after that we skirted wheat and turnip fields, because when we tried to cross them, as we were not sportsmen, there was some one near at hand to stop us. We went up and down ravines, and picked our way through tall grass at the very edge of sheer cliffs. The afternoon was hotter than the morning had been. A warm haze hung over the level stretch of country and the distant hills. The sky seemed to have fallen down upon the sea; there was not a line to mark where it met the water. The few

BIT OF MACDUFF.

brown-sailed boats looked as if they were forcing their way between, holding up the heavens on their masts.

In one place, on a high rock jutting out into the sea, was a low broken wall of rough masonry, all that is left of Findlater Castle.

There was no use in trying to keep up any longer. Our backs ached, our shoulders were cut; we were hot, dusty, exhausted, and, in a word, at the end of our physical and moral forces. This scramble on the cliffs ended our walking tour.

At Sandend we took the train for Banff; but first we went down to the shore; for Sandend was a picturesque little village, with all its gables turned towards the sea, big black boats on the beach, rocks beyond, and a pretty blue bay of its own. Three artists had left their easels to eat buns out of a brown-paper bag and drink beer out of bottles, under the shade of one of the boats. J——, having already learned the exclusiveness of British artists, took out his sketch-book at a safe distance. He only spoke to them to ask the way to the station. He did not dare to talk about work.

A little farther on we again asked the way, this time of a girl hanging up clothes. J——'s questions and her answers were typical of many conversations, bad for one's temper, that we held on the east coast.

"Where is the railway-station?"

"What station?"

"Where the train comes in."

"There;" and she pointed to a house beyond the village.

"How do you get there?"

"By the road."

"Can you go up by the hill?"

"Yes."

"Which is better?"

"I don't know."

"Which is shorter?"

"Up the hill."

We started up the hill, but there was no path. "There is no path," we said to her.

"No, there's no path."

We came to

BANFF

late in the afternoon, just as the fishing-boats were putting out to sea, one beyond another on the gray water, the farthest but faint specks on the horizon. The best thing about Banff is that in fifteen or twenty minutes you can be out of it and in Macduff. The shore here makes a great curve. On one point is Banff, on the other Macduff; half-way between, a many-arched bridge spans the river Deveron, and close by the big house of the Earl of Fife shows through the trees of his park. High on the hill of Macduff stands the white kirk; it overlooks the town, with its many rows of fishermen's houses, and the harbor, where the black masts rise far above the gray walls, and the fishermen spread out their nets to dry, and the dark-sailed boats are always coming and going, and boys paddle in the twilight. And if you go to the far end of the harbor, where the light-house is, you look to the spires and chimneys and roofs of Banff climbing up their hill-side, and beyond to a shadowy point of land like a pale gray cloud-bank on the water.

It was easy to see what they thought of us at

the Fife Arms, where we stayed in Banff. We were given our breakfast with the nurse and children of an A. R. A., while the great man breakfasted in state in a near dining-room. They ate

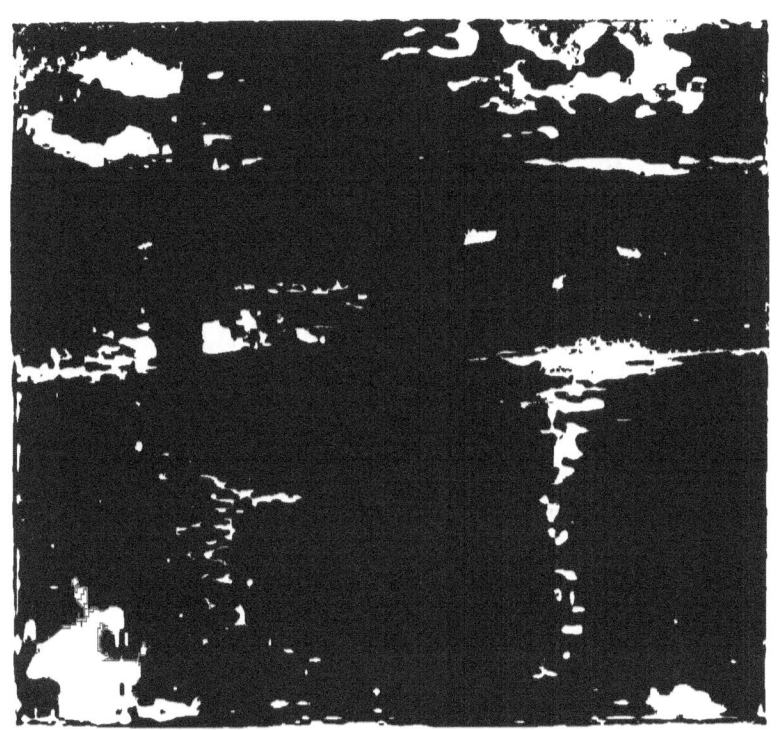

NEAR BANFF.

very like ordinary children, but their clothes showed them to be little boys and girls of æsthetic distinction. I fear, however, we were not properly impressed.

There was no doubt that now our walking was

13

all done. We asked about the stage for Fraserburgh, as if staging with us was a matter of course. It was a relief not to begin the day by strapping heavy knapsacks to our backs. The hours of waiting were spent partly in strolling through the streets of Banff, where here and there is an old gray house with pretty turret at its corner, or quaint old inscription with coat of arms or figures let into its walls; partly in sitting on the beach looking out on a hot blue sea.

But hot as it was in the morning, a sharp, cold wind was blowing when, at three o'clock, we took our seats in the little old-fashioned stage that runs between Banff and Fraserburgh. Stage and coachman and passengers seemed like a page out of Dickens transposed to Scotland. Inside was a very small boy, put there by a fat woman in black, and left, with many exhortations and a couple of buns, to make the journey alone; opposite to him sat a melancholy man who saw but ruin staring in the face of farmers and fishermen alike. At every corner in Banff and Macduff we stopped for more passengers, until the stage, elastic as it seemed, was full to overflowing, and we took refuge on the top. Here the seats were crowded with men, their heads tied up in scarfs. The coachman was carrier as well, and at different points in the open country women and children waited by the road to give him, or to take from him, bundles

BANFF, FROM MACDUFF.

and boxes and letters. He was the typical cheery carrier. He had a word for everybody, even for a young man who dropped his wheelbarrow to flap his arms and greet us with a vacant smile. He was a puir thing, the driver explained, who went wrong only four years ago. He was the third we had seen in two days.

Many of the carrier's jokes we lost. A commercial traveller, who sat next to us, supposed we could not understand some of the expressions hereabouts. He might better have said we could not understand the language. We could make out enough, however, to find that one joke went a long way. A man in the front seat, trying to light his pipe in the wind, set off the whole box of matches. "That's extravagance," said the carrier; and when another box was handed to the man, he told him that these were safety matches—it took only one to light a pipe; and this he kept saying over and over again, with many chuckles, for the next half-hour. We had a specimen, too, of Scotch humor. At one stopping-place the commercial traveller got down and went into the public-house. A family party scrambled up and filled every seat, his with the rest. J—— remonstrated; but the man of the party answered that he paid his money for a seat as well as anybody else. "An empty seat's naebody's seat," he argued, and carrier and passengers roared at his fun.

The country was dreary, for all its cultivation. The fields were without tree or hedge to break their monotony. The villages were full of new houses. There was nothing striking or picturesque until we came within sight of Fraserburgh. Far across a level stretch we first saw it, its spires rising high above gray and red roofs. The near meadows were dark with fishing-nets; in places fishermen were at work spreading them over the grass; and we began to pass carts heavily laden with their brown masses, and men and women bent under the same burdens.

FRASERBURGH.

We walked out after supper. Rain was falling, and the evening was growing dark. Down by the harbor carts were still going and coming; men were still busy with their nets. Along the quay was a succession of basins, and these opened into others beyond. All were crowded with boats, and their thickly clustered masts seemed, in the gathering shadows, like a forest of branchless, leafless trees. One by one lights were hung out. On the town side of the quay, in crypt-like rooms and under low sheds, torches flamed and flared against a background of darkness. Their strong light fell upon women clothed in strange stuffs that glistened and glittered, their heads bound with white cloths. They were bending over shiny, ever-shifting masses piled at their feet, and chanting a wild

FRASERBURGH.

Gaelic song that rose and fell with the wailing of all savage music. As we first saw them, from a distance, they might have been so many sorceresses at their magic rites. When we drew near we found that they were but the fish-curers' gutters and packers at work. Thanks to Cable and Lafcadio Hearn, we know something of the songs of work at home; but who in England cares about the singing in these fishing towns—singing which is only wilder and weirder than that of the cotton pressers of Louisiana? To the English literary man, however—the Charles Reades are the exceptions—I fear the gutters would be but nasty, dirty fisher persons. Now and then groups of these women passed us, walking with long strides, their arms swinging, and their short skirts and white-bound heads shining through the sombre streets. Over the town was the glow of the many fires.

In the morning there was less mystery, but not less picturesqueness. We were up in time to go to the harbor with the fishermen's wives, and watch the boats come in. Everything was fresh after a night of rain. It was still early, and the sun sent a path of gold across the sea just where the boats turned on their last tack homeward. Each brown sail was set in bold relief against the shining east, and then slowly lowered, as the fishermen with their long poles pushed the boats into the already crowded harbor. At once nets were emptied of the fish, which lay gleaming like silver through the brown meshes. Women and boys came to fill baskets with the fresh herrings; carts were loaded with them. In other boats men were hanging up their floats and shaking out their nets. The water was rich with the many black and brown reflections, only brightened here and there by lines of blue or purple or white from the distinguishing rings of color on each mast. There was a never-ending stream of men and carts passing along the quay. Many fishermen with their bags were on their way to the station, for the fishing season was almost over. So they said. But when one thousand boats came in, and twenty thousand fisher-folk were that day in Fraserburgh, to us it looked little like the end. In all this busy place we heard no English. Only Gaelic was spoken, as if we were once more in the Western Islands.

It was the same in the streets. The day's work in the curing-houses was just about to begin. Girls and women in groups of threes and fours were walking towards them. In the morning light we could see that the greater number were young. All were neat and clean, with hair carefully parted and well brushed, little shawls over their shoulders, but nothing on their heads. They carried their working clothes under their arms, and kept knitting as they walked. Like the men, they all talked Gaelic.

IN THE HARBOR, FRASERBURGH.

When they got to work, we found that those strange stuffs which had glistened in the torch-light were aprons and bibs smeared with scales and slime, that the white head-dresses were worn only for cleanliness, that the shining masses at their feet were but piles of herring. I have never seen women work so hard or so fast. Their arms, as they seized the fish, gutted them, and threw them in the buckets, moved with the regularity and the speed of machines. Indeed, there could not be a busier place than Fraserburgh. All day long the boats kept coming in, nets were emptied, fish carted away. The harbor, the streets, the fields beyond where nets were taken to dry, the curing-houses, were alike scenes of industry. If the women put down their knives, it was only to take up their knitting. And yet these men and women, working incessantly by day and by night, were almost all Western Islanders—the people who, we are told, are so slovenly and so lazy! No one who comes with them to the east coast for the fishing season will ever again believe in the oft-repeated lies about their idleness.

There were no signs of rest until Saturday evening. Then no boats went out, and the harbor and curing-houses were deserted. The streets were full of men and women walking about for pleasure. The greatest crowd was in the market-place, where a few "cheap Jacks" drove their trade. Two, who dealt in china, as if to make up for their poor patter, threw cups and saucers recklessly into the air, breaking them with great clatter, while the women and girls they had attracted stood by and bought nothing.

The fishermen had gathered about a third, who sold cheap and tawdry ornaments, but who could patter. When we first came near he was holding up six imitation gold watch-chains, and offering the buyers prizes into the bargain. "O ye men of little faith!"—shaking his fist at them—"can't any of you favor me with a shillin'? You don't want 'em, gen'lemen? Then there'll be smashin' of teeth and tearin' of hair. Glory! glory hallylujah!" All this, I regret to say, was interspersed with stories that do not bear repetition. But he sold his watch-chains without trouble. "And now, gen'lemen, for any of you that wants to take home a present to your wife and chil'ren, here's an album. It'd adorn a nobleman's mansion, and wouldn't disgrace a fisherman's cottage. It's bound in moroccer and stamped with gold, and 'll hold many pictures. I'll only sell half a dozen, and it's the very thing you wants. You'll have one? Well, sir, I can't reach you, but these gen'lemen 'll pass it along."

And then he began again with the stories and the Scripture until he had sold out all his stock of albums and note-books and cheap jewellery.

GUTTERS AT WORK, FRASERBURGH.

It was the hint about presents to those left behind which bore greatest weight with the fishermen. It never failed. But we remembered their cottages and the sadness of their homes, and it angered us that they should be duped into wasting their hard-won earnings on tawdry ornaments. It seems to be their fate to be cheated by every one. Even the peddler, like the parson and the landlord, can pervert Scripture to their discomfort.

Still, there was a pleasant suggestion of holiday-making in the square. It was the first time we had seen the Western Islanders amusing themselves. True, they did it very solemnly. There was little laughter and much silence; but at least a touch of brightness was given to the gloom of their long life of work and want.

Even on Sunday we thought the people more cheerful. In the morning the women, the little shawls over their shoulders, their heads still bare, the men in blue cloth, many without coats, again filled the streets on their way to church. In the afternoon we walked to two near fishing villages. In one an old fisherman was talking about Christ to a few villagers. We sat a while close to the sea, looking out to the next village, gray against gray gold-lined clouds, to the water with the light falling softly across it, to the little quiet pools in among the low rocks of the shore, to the big black boats drawn up on the beach. And then, as we walked back to Fraserburgh, the mist fell suddenly. But the road near the town was crowded with the men in blue cloth and the women in short skirts. Some were singing hymns as they walked. To us they looked strong and healthy, and even happy. It seemed as if this life on the east coast must make up for many of the hardships they endure in the deserts of their western home.

That same evening in the hotel we heard about life in Fraserburgh, which looks so prosperous to the stranger. A Catholic priest came into the dining-room after supper. He seemed very tired. He had been visiting the sick all day, he told us. Measles had broken out among the women and girls from the Hebrides. Many had already died; more had been carried to the hospital. The rooms provided for them by the curers were small and overcrowded. So long as they were kept in their present quarters, so long would disease and death be their portion. Their condition was dreadful; but they worked hard, and never complained. He came from the west coast of Ireland, he said, where Irish poverty is at its worst, but not even there had he seen misery as great as that of the Western Islanders. He knew it well. He had lived with them in the Long Island, where many are Catholics. If the Highlands were represented by eighty-five members, all wanting Home Rule, more would have been heard about destitution in the Hebrides.

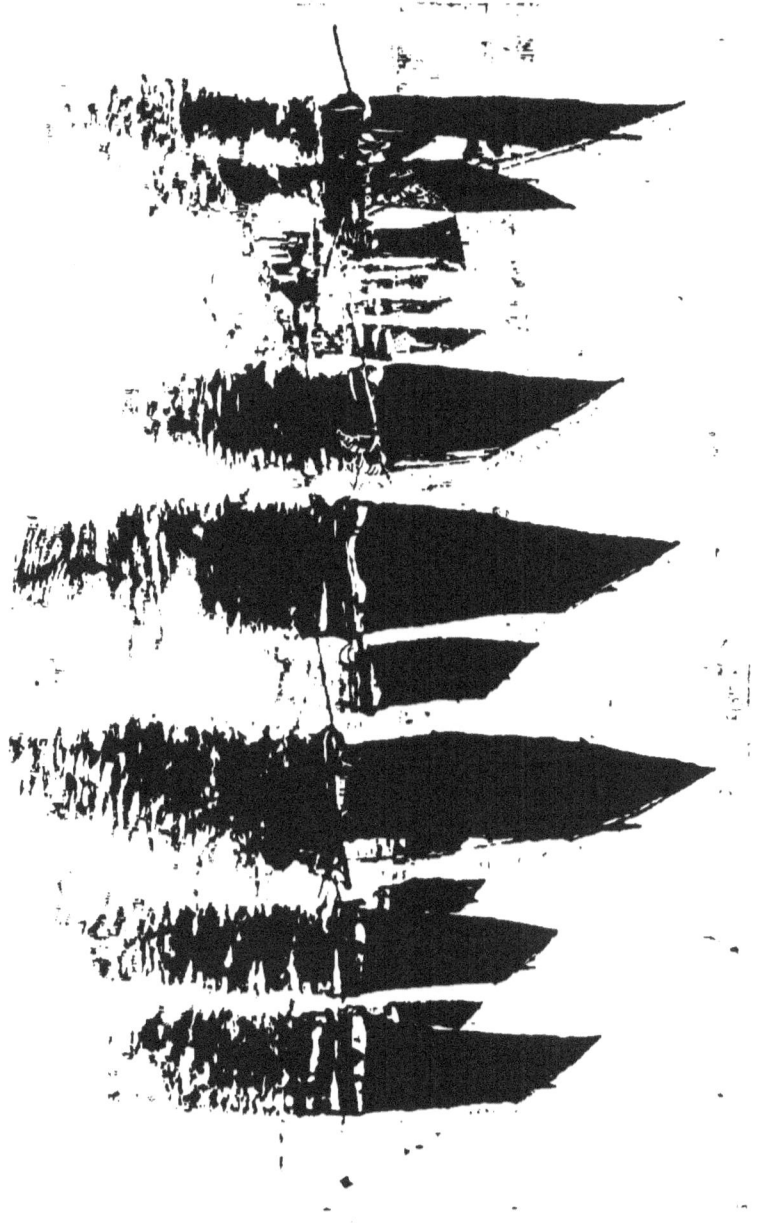

COMING HOME FROM THE FISHERIES, FRASERBURGH.

In the prosperous days of the east coast fisheries the people's burden had been less heavy; but now they came to the fishing towns of the east, the women to sicken and to die, the men to beg their way back as best they could. There were too many fishermen here, just as at home landlords thought there were too many crofters.

The fishers also shall mourn, and all they that cast angle shall lament, and they that spread nets upon the waters shall languish.

The epidemic and its causes became the town talk. The Gaelic Free Kirk minister, differ as he might from the Catholic priest on every other point, on this could but agree with him. He told us the same story in words as strong. It was shameful, he said, the way these poor girls were being killed. He had not known it before; but now that he did, he could not and would not let the matter rest. An indignation meeting of the people of Fraserburgh was called for the day we left. The town was placarded with the notices. Since then the report must have gone abroad. Now that agitation in Lewis is forcing attention to the islands and their people, in London there has been formed a committee of *ladies* to look into the condition of the girls and women who work on the east coast.

That last morning, as we stood by the hotel door, the funeral of one of the dead women passed up the street towards the station. Fifty or sixty fishermen followed the coffin. When we took our seats in a third-class carriage we found the Free Kirk minister there before us. The coffin had just been put on the train. Two girls came up to speak to him. He stretched out his hand; one took and held it as she struggled to answer his questions; the other turned away with the tears streaming down her face. As the train started they stood apart, their heads bent low, their faces buried in their shawls, both crying as if their hearts would break. And so, at the last, we saw only the sadness of Fraserburgh.

We had intended going to Peterhead and the smaller fishing towns by the way; but our energy was less inexhaustible than the picturesqueness of the east coast. Our journey had been over-long. We were beginning to be anxious to bring it to an end. Now we went straight to

ABERDEEN,

where we at once fell back into ordinary city life. We even did a little shopping in its fine new streets. Its large harbor seemed empty after that of Fraserburgh. Many fishing-boats were at sea; many had gone altogether. The fishing season here was really well over. We walked to the old town after dinner. In it there is not much to be seen but the university tower with the famous

ENTRANCE TO THE HARBOR AT MONTROSE.

crown atop, and the cathedral, which looked massive and impressive in the twilight. We saw much more of Aberdeen; but we are quite of the same mind as Dr. Johnson, that to write of such well-known cities "with the solemnity of geographical description, as if we had been cast upon a newly discovered coast, has the appearance of a very frivolous ostentation."

From Aberdeen to Edinburgh we trained it by easy stages. We stopped often; once at

MONTROSE,

where, like Dr. Johnson, and for that matter, every one else who comes here, we looked to the Grampian Hills in the distance. The town itself was not picturesque. The guide-book calls it neat and Flemish, probably because it has fewer houses with high gables turned towards the street than can be seen, as a rule, in any Scotch town. But the harbor, of which the guide-book says less, was fine. We spent hours near the mouth of the river, looking over to the fishermen's houses on the opposite shore. There were constant showers as we sat there; every few minutes the sun came out from the clouds, and the wet roofs glistened and glittered through the smoke hanging above them. In the morning, women, packed like herrings in the huge ferry-boats, crossed over to the curing-houses. Now and then a fishing-boat sailed slowly in.

One sees little from the cars. Of the country through which we passed I remember only occasional glimpses of the sea and of fishing villages and of red castles, which made us wish we were still on the road. Now and then, as we sat comfortably in the railway-carriage, we determined to walk back to see them, or to get a tricycle at Edinburgh and "do" the whole east coast over again; but we always left our determinations with the carriage. Of all the places at which we stopped, I remember best

ARBROATH,

the sight of which seemed worth his whole journey to Dr. Johnson. Little is left of the abbey save the broken walls and towers. A street runs through the old gate-house. The public park and children's play-ground lie to one side of the ruined church. A few old tombs and tablets and bits of ornament have been gathered together in the sacristy, which is in better preservation than the rest of the building. We found them less interesting than the guide who explained them. He gave a poetical touch to the usual verger recitation, and indeed to all his talk, of which there was plenty. 'Twas better to have loved and lost, than never to have loved at all, was his manner of expressing regret for the loss of an old engraving of the abbey. There were many hard things in this world, but grass was soft; why, then, should I choose the hard things? was his way of inviting me to walk on the grass instead of the gravel. But it was not until he showed us the original copy, full of blots and corrections, of one of Burns's poems that we found he too was a poet—a successful poet, it seemed, for he had sold 14,000 copies of his volume of poems—very few, he thought. If he were a member of the London Society of Authors he would know better. He had given the last copy to William Morris, when the latter was in the town. William Morris did not wear gaudy clothes, not he. He looked like a sailor in his blue flannel shirt, and there was a slit in his hat. And when he returned to London he sent his "Jason" to his fellow-poet in Arbroath.

As we were leaving, he told us how, one day, two ladies had driven up to the abbey, looked at nothing, but at once asked him to recite his "Abbey Gate." He did so, and then, without a word, they slipped a guinea into his hand, and there were tears on their cheeks. He never knew who they were. After this, we felt our tribute to be very small; but he clasped our hands warmly at parting. There was something out of the common in our faces, he said.

We talked to no one else in Arbroath, except to a pessimistic stationer. While we bought his paper he grumbled because farmers could not sell their cattle and corn. Some people said the country needed protection ; " but, sir, what have we got to protect ?"

Of the rest of the journey to Edinburgh my note-book says nothing, and little remains in my memory. But I know that when we walked up from the station to Waverley Bridge, and looked to the gray precipice of houses of the Old Town, we realized that our long wanderings had not shown us anything so fine.

And now our journey was at an end. Like Dr. Johnson's, it began and finished in Edinburgh, but it resembled his in little else. From the start, we continually took liberties with his route; we often forgot that he was our guide. We went to places he had never seen; we turned our backs upon many through which he and Boswell had travelled. But at least he had helped us to form definite plans without weeks of hard map-study which they otherwise must have cost us.

We had come back wiser in many ways. In the first place, we had learned that for us walking on a tour of this kind, or indeed of any kind, is a mistake. Had we never cycled, perhaps we might not have felt this so keenly. Our powers of endurance are not, I think, below the average; but the power to endure so many miles a day on foot is very different from the capacity to enjoy them; and if on such a trip one proposes, as we did, to work, without pleasure in the exercise, how can

RUINS AT ARBROATH.

one hope for good results? But for the two days' coaching on the west coast, the necessary steaming among the islands, our utter collapse on the east coast, I am sure we never should have worked at all. Day after day we were dispirited, disheartened, and only happy when we were not walking. We went to bed in the evening and got up in the morning wearied and exhausted. The usual walking tours of which one hears mean a day's climbing in the mountains, or a day's tramp with bag or knapsack sent before by train or stage. Under these conditions we probably would not be the first to give in. But to be as independent as if on a tricycle, to have one's sketching traps when needed, one must carry a knapsack one's self. J——'s weighed between twenty-five and thirty pounds; mine, fifteen. Never before have I appreciated so well the true significance of Christian's burden. But even worse than this constant strain on our shoulders was the monotony of our pace. Whether the road was good or bad, level or hilly, there was no change, no relief. In cycling, for one hard day's work you know you will have two of pleasure. As for short-cuts, they are, as a rule, out of the question. One does not know the country through which one is passing; it is the exception to meet a native. After cycling more thousands of miles than we have walked hundreds, we know it to be not mere theorizing when we declare that no comparison between the two methods of travelling is possible. One is just enough work to make the pleasure greater; the other is all work.

Our experience has taught us to be sceptical about the tramps of other days who saw Europe afoot. We wonder if they told the whole story. Of modern tramps, none has given such a delightful record as has Mr. Stevenson of the walk he took with a donkey through the Cevennes. And yet, even with him, if you read between his lines, or, for that matter, the lines themselves, you realize that, charming as his story is for us, the reality for him was wearisome, depressing, and often painful, and that probably to it is to be referred much of his after physical weakness. We have also had a new light thrown upon the life of tramps at home, who are so often supposed to have chosen the better part. Theirs is as much a life of toil as if they broke stones on the same roads over which they journey. They are not to be envied, but pitied. The next time one begs from you as he passes, give him something out of your charity; he deserves it.

However, many drawbacks as there were to our walk, we do not regret it. In no other way could we have come to know the country and the people with the same friendly intimacy. For pure enjoyment, it would be best to go over the greater part of our route in a yacht. From it is to be seen much beauty and little misery. The coast-line can be followed, excursions made inland. But a yacht is a luxury for the rich. Besides, on it one lives one's own life, not that of the country one has come to visit. On foot, with knapsacks on our backs, we often passed for peddlers. Certainly we were never mistaken to be tourists of means or sportsmen. Therefore the people met us as equals and talked to us freely.

We were able to correct the vague and false impressions with which we had started. If we did not master the geography of all Scotland, I think—at least on the two coasts as far north as the Caledonian Canal—we could now pass an examination with credit. We learned that haggis and oatmeal figure more extensively in books than on hotel tables; the first we saw not at all, the second but twice, and then it was not offered to us.

Above all, we learned the burden of Scotland, whose Highlands have been laid waste, their people brought to silence. But now the people themselves have broken their long silence, and a cry has gone up from them against their oppressors. If by telling exactly what we saw we can in the least strengthen that cry, we shall feel that our journeying has not been in vain.

THE END.

By WILLIAM BLACK.

HARPER'S LIBRARY EDITION.

12mo, Cloth, $1 25 per volume.

A DAUGHTER OF HETH.
A PRINCESS OF THULE.
GREEN PASTURES AND PICCADILLY.
IN FAR LOCHABER.
IN SILK ATTIRE.
JUDITH SHAKESPEARE. Ill'd.
KILMENY.
MACLEOD OF DARE. Illustrated.
MADCAP VIOLET.
SABINA ZEMBRA.
SHANDON BELLS. Illustrated.
SUNRISE.
THAT BEAUTIFUL WRETCH. Ill'd.
THE STRANGE ADVENTURES OF A HOUSE-BOAT. Illustrated.
THE STRANGE ADVENTURES OF A PHAETON.
THREE FEATHERS.
WHITE HEATHER.
WHITE WINGS.
YOLANDE. Illustrated.

HARPER'S POPULAR EDITION.

A DAUGHTER OF HETH. 8vo, Paper, 35 cents.
A PRINCESS OF THULE. 8vo, Paper, 50 cents.
AN ADVENTURE IN THULE. 4to, Paper, 10 cents.
GREEN PASTURES AND PICCADILLY. 8vo, Paper, 50 cents.
IN FAR LOCHABER. 8vo, Paper, 40 cents.
IN SILK ATTIRE. 8vo, Paper, 35 cents.
JUDITH SHAKESPEARE. 4to, Paper, 20 cents.
KILMENY. 8vo, Paper, 35 cents.
MACLEOD OF DARE. 8vo, Paper, Ill'd, 60 cts.; 4to, Paper, 15 cts.
MADCAP VIOLET. 8vo, Paper, 50 cents.
SABINA ZEMBRA. 4to, Paper, 20 cents.
SHANDON BELLS. Illustrated. 4to, Paper, 20 cents.
SUNRISE. 4to, Paper, 20 cents.
THAT BEAUTIFUL WRETCH. Illustrated. 4to, Paper, 20 cents.
THE MAID OF KILLEENA, THE MARRIAGE OF MOIRA FERGUS, and Other Stories. 8vo, Paper, 40 cents.
THE MONARCH OF MINCING-LANE. Ill'd. 8vo, Paper, 50 cts.
THE STRANGE ADVENTURES OF A HOUSE-BOAT. Illustrated. 8vo, Paper, 50 cents.
THE STRANGE ADVENTURES OF A PHAETON. 8vo, Paper, 50 cts.
THREE FEATHERS. Illustrated. 8vo, Paper, 50 cents.
WHITE HEATHER. 4to, Paper, 20 cents.
WHITE WINGS. 4to, Paper, 20 cts.
YOLANDE. Illustrated. 4to, Paper, 20 cents.
THE FOUR MACNICOLS. Ill'd. Square 16mo, Cloth, $1 00.

Published by HARPER & BROTHERS, New York.

☞ *Any of the above works sent by mail, postage prepaid, to any part of the United States, Canada, or Mexico, on receipt of the price.*

By CHAS. DUDLEY WARNER.

STUDIES IN THE SOUTH AND WEST, with Comments on Canada. pp. iv., 484. Post 8vo, Half Leather. (*Just Ready.*)

THEIR PILGRIMAGE. Richly Illustrated by C. S. REINHART. pp. viii., 364. Post 8vo, Half Leather, $2 00.

Aside from the delicious story—its wonderful portraitures of character and its dramatic development—the book is precious to all who know anything about the great American watering-places, for it contains incomparable descriptions of those famous resorts and their frequenters. Even without the aid of Mr. Reinhart's brilliant drawings, Mr. Warner conjures up word-pictures of Cape May, Newport, Saratoga, Lake George, Richfield Springs, Niagara, the White Mountains, and all the rest, which strike the eye like photographs, so clear is every outline. But Mr. Reinhart's designs fit into the text so closely that we could not bear to part with a single one of them.—*N. Y. Journal of Commerce.*

The author touches the canvas here and there with lines of color that fix and identify American character.... Of the fancy and humor of Mr. Warner, which in witchery of their play and power are quite independent of this or that subject, there is nothing to add. But acknowledgment is due Mr. Reinhart for nearly eighty finely conceived drawings, and to the publishers for the substantial and rich letter-press and covers.—*Boston Globe.*

Mr. Warner's pen-pictures of the characters typical of each resort, of the manner of life followed at each, of the humor and absurdities peculiar to Saratoga, or Newport, or Bar Harbor, as the case may be, are as good-natured as they are clever. The satire, when there is any, is of the mildest, and the general tone is that of one glad to look on the brightest side of the cheerful, pleasure-seeking world with which he mingles.... In Mr. Reinhart the author has an assistant who has done with his pencil almost exactly what Mr. Warner has accomplished with his pen. His drawings are spirited, catch with wonderful success the tone and costume of each place visited, and abound in good-natured fun.—*Christian Union, N. Y.*

Mr. Reinhart's spirited and realistic illustrations are very attractive, and contribute to make an unusually handsome book. We have already commented upon the earlier chapters of the text; and the happy blending of travel and fiction which we looked forward to with confidence did, in fact, distinguish this story among the serials of the year.—*N. Y. Evening Post.*

PUBLISHED BY HARPER & BROTHERS, NEW YORK.

☞ *Either of the above works sent by mail, postage prepaid, to any part of the United States, Canada, or Mexico, on receipt of the price.*

By W. D. HOWELLS.

MODERN ITALIAN POETS. Essays and Versions. With Portraits. 12mo, Half Cloth, $2 00.

APRIL HOPES. 12mo, Cloth, $1 50.

ANNIE KILBURN. 12mo, Cloth, $1 50.

THE MOUSE-TRAP, and Other Farces. Illustrated. 12mo, Cloth, $1 00.

A portfolio of delightsome studies among the Italian poets; musings in a golden granary full to the brim with good things.... We venture to say that no acute and penetrating critic surpasses Mr. Howells in true insight, in polished irony, in effective and yet graceful treatment of his theme, in that light and indescribable touch that lifts you over a whole sea of froth and foam, and fixes your eye, not on the froth and foam, but on the solid objects, the true heart and soul of the theme.—*Critic*, N. Y.

A more companionable, entertaining, stimulating work than this book has not been printed for many a day. It is a book to be studied privately, to be read aloud, to be cherished and quoted and reread many times, and every reader of it will cry for more translations from the Italian by the same delight-conferring pen.—*Chicago Tribune*.

This is a noble volume, the fruit of studies begun twenty years ago in Italy.... The subject is discussed with all the rare fascination of style and thought which Mr. Howells is so well qualified to bring to it, and the volume will be treasured by every lover of poetry of whatever period or clime.—*Christian at Work*, N. Y.

No living writer could give us this picture of a literary movement with such delicacy of appreciation and discrimination. The period embraced is about a century; the names selected comprise all the poets which a survey of the movement, now over, distinguishes as principal factors in it.—*Hartford Courant*.

"April Hopes" is a specimen of Mr. Howells's well-known consummate art as a delineator of young men and maidens, and a chronicler of all the fluctuations of love affairs. From the life-like description of Harvard Class Day and its participants, in the opening chapters, to the conclusion of the story, Mr. Howells is at his best.—*N. Y. Journal of Commerce*.

Mr. Howells never wrote a more bewitching book. It is useless to deny the rarity and worth of the skill that can report so perfectly and with such exquisite humor all the fugacious and manifold emotions of the modern maiden and her lover.—*Philadelphia Press*.

PUBLISHED BY HARPER & BROTHERS, NEW YORK.

☞ *Any of the above works sent by mail, postage prepaid, to any part of the United States or Canada, on receipt of the price.*

By CONSTANCE F. WOOLSON.

EAST ANGELS. pp. 592. 16mo, Cloth, $1 25.

ANNE. Illustrated. pp. 540. 16mo, Cloth, $1 25.

FOR THE MAJOR. pp. 208. 16mo, Cloth, $1 00.

CASTLE NOWHERE. pp. 386. 16mo, Cloth, $1 00. (*A New Edition.*)

RODMAN THE KEEPER. Southern Sketches. pp. 340. 16mo, Cloth, $1 00. (*A New Edition.*)

There is a certain bright cheerfulness in Miss Woolson's writing which invests all her characters with lovable qualities.—*Jewish Advocate*, N. Y.

Miss Woolson is among our few successful writers of interesting magazine stories, and her skill and power are perceptible in the delineation of her heroines no less than in the suggestive pictures of local life.—*Jewish Messenger*, N. Y.

Constance Fenimore Woolson may easily become the novelist laureate.—*Boston Globe.*

Miss Woolson has a graceful fancy, a ready wit, a polished style, and conspicuous dramatic power; while her skill in the development of a story is very remarkable.—*London Life.*

Miss Woolson never once follows the beaten track of the orthodox novelist, but strikes a new and richly loaded vein, which so far is all her own; and thus we feel, on reading one of her works, a fresh sensation, and we put down the book with a sigh to think our pleasant task of reading it is finished. The author's lines must have fallen to her in very pleasant places; or she has, perhaps, within herself the wealth of womanly love and tenderness she pours so freely into all she writes. Such books as hers do much to elevate the moral tone of the day—a quality sadly wanting in novels of the time.—*Whitehall Review*, London.

PUBLISHED BY HARPER & BROTHERS, NEW YORK.

☞ *The above works sent by mail, postage prepaid, to any part of the United States or Canada, on receipt of the price.*

By AMÉLIE RIVES.

A BROTHER TO DRAGONS, AND OTHER OLD-TIME TALES. Post 8vo, Cloth, Extra, $1 00.

VIRGINIA OF VIRGINIA. A Story. Illustrated. Post 8vo, Cloth, Extra, $1 00.

One is permitted to discover qualities of mind and a proficiency and capacity in art from which something new and distinctively the work of genius may be anticipated in American literature.—*Boston Globe.*

Miss Rives has imagination, breadth, and a daring and courage oftenest spoken of as masculine. Moreover, she is exquisitely poetical, and her ideals, with all the mishaps of her delineations, are of an exalted order.—*N. Y. Star.*

It was little more than two years ago that Miss Rives made her first literary conquest, a conquest so complete and astonishing as at once to give her fame. How well she has sustained and added to the reputation she so suddenly won, we all know, and the permanency of that reputation demonstrates conclusively that her success did not depend upon the lucky striking of a popular fancy, but that it rests upon enduring qualities that are developing more and more richly year by year.—*Richmond State.*

It is evident that the author has imagination in an unusual degree, much strength of expression, and skill in delineating character.—*Boston Journal.*

There are few young writers who begin a promising career with so much spontaneity and charm of expression as is displayed by Miss Rives.—*Literary World*, Boston.

The trait which the author seems to take the most pleasure in depicting is the passionate loyalty of a girl to her lover or of a young wife to her husband, and her portrayal of this trait has feeling, and is set off by an unconventional style and brisk movement.—*The Book Buyer*, N. Y.

There is such a wealth of imagination, such an exuberance of striking language in the productions of this author, as to attract and hold the reader.—*Toledo Blade.*

Miss Rives is essentially a teller of love stories, and relates them with such simple, straightforward grace that she at once captures the sympathy and interest of the reader. . . . There is a freshness of feeling and a mingling of pathos and humor which are simply delicious.—*New London Telegraph.*

PUBLISHED BY HARPER & BROTHERS, NEW YORK.

☞ HARPER & BROTHERS *will send either of the above works by mail, postage prepaid, to any part of the United States or Canada, on receipt of the price.*

BEN-HUR: A TALE OF THE CHRIST.

By LEW. WALLACE. New Edition from New Electrotype Plates. pp. 560. 16mo, Cloth, $1 50; Half Calf, $3 00.

Anything so startling, new, and distinctive as the leading feature of this romance does not often appear in works of fiction.... Some of Mr. Wallace's writing is remarkable for its pathetic eloquence. The scenes described in the New Testament are re-written with the power and skill of an accomplished master of style.—*N. Y. Times.*

Its real basis is a description of the life of the Jews and Romans at the beginning of the Christian era, and this is both forcible and brilliant.... We are carried through a surprising variety of scenes; we witness a sea-fight, a chariot-race, the internal economy of a Roman galley, domestic interiors at Antioch, at Jerusalem, and among the tribes of the desert: palaces, prisons, the haunts of dissipated Roman youth, the houses of pious families of Israel. There is plenty of exciting incident; everything is animated, vivid, and glowing.—*N. Y. Tribune.*

From the opening of the volume to the very close the reader's interest will be kept at the highest pitch, and the novel will be pronounced by all one of the greatest novels of the day.—*Boston Post.*

It is full of poetic beauty, as though born of an Eastern sage, and there is sufficient of Oriental customs, geography, nomenclature, etc., to greatly strengthen the semblance.—*Boston Commonwealth.*

"Ben-Hur" is interesting, and its characterization is fine and strong. Meanwhile it evinces careful study of the period in which the scene is laid, and will help those who read it with reasonable attention to realize the nature and conditions of Hebrew life in Jerusalem and Roman life at Antioch at the time of our Saviour's advent.—*Examiner, N. Y.*

It is really Scripture history of Christ's time, clothed gracefully and delicately in the flowing and loose drapery of modern fiction.... Few late works of fiction excel it in genuine ability and interest.—*N. Y. Graphic.*

One of the most remarkable and delightful books. It is as real and warm as life itself, and as attractive as the grandest and most heroic chapters of history.—*Indianapolis Journal.*

The book is one of unquestionable power, and will be read with unwonted interest by many readers who are weary of the conventional novel and romance.—*Boston Journal.*

PUBLISHED BY HARPER & BROTHERS, NEW YORK.

☞ *The above work sent by mail, postage prepaid, to any part of the United States or Canada, on receipt of the price.*

www.ingramcontent.com/pod-product-compliance
Lightning Source LLC
Chambersburg PA
CBHW031730230426
43669CB00007B/310